Progressive Faith and Practice

Progressive Faith and Practice

Thou Shalt Not Stand Idly By

Roger L. Ray

Foreword by
Charles W. Hedrick

WIPF & STOCK · Eugene, Oregon

Wipf and Stock
An Imprint of Wipf and Stock Publishers
199 W. 8th Ave., Suite 3
Eugene, OR 97401

www.wipfandstock.com

ISBN 13: 978-1-62564-846-4

Manufactured in the U.S.A.   07/14/2014

Contents

Foreword

TRADITIONS ABOUT JESUS OF Nazareth have never been uniform. The earliest written sources, appearing more than a generation after the death of Jesus, portray the earlier first-century man in similar, yet different and contradictory ways. The canonical gospels (Mark, Matthew, Luke, and John) clearly describe him as an heir of the Israelite religion growing up under the influence of the Judean state religion and its temple at Jerusalem. He had a small group of associates, whom the gospel writers called "disciples." They described his debates with the priests of the temple and other groups over the issue of the interpretation of the Israelite law. Some few years later other written sources describe the followers of Jesus as heirs of Greco-Roman culture. Charismatic leaders like Paul brought them together in small local "gatherings of holy ones" (i.e., saints). Paul and his small "gatherings" expected an immediate end to the world. It did not come, however, and as they waited they developed rituals, hymns, and confessions, drawing their personal ethics from Roman culture, rather than from Jesus.

It soon became apparent that the world was not going to end immediately, and that their view of themselves as "gatherings of the end time" had to be modified. Among the innovations was the addition of a collection of new writings to the Hebrew scriptures, which had been the scriptures for Jesus and Paul. These new writings, which included a number of Paul's letters to his gatherings of saints, were described as "New Covenant" writings, as opposed to the "Old Covenant" Israelite scriptures, which were no longer meeting their religious needs. They were, after all, no longer

Hebrews or Israelites, but "Christians," who required literature more appropriate to their new faith.

The Christian church has never been unified. It was comprised in the middle of the first century of diverse groups reflecting different practices, theologies, and creeds, and that diversity has continued to be the case. A number of church councils were held in the fourth through the eighth centuries attempting to reduce the diversity and bring unity to the church, but diversity has plagued Christianity from its very beginning. Indeed, Christian faith has always been nourished in the fertile soil of diversity.

One might surmise that at the very least they held a common faith in Jesus, but it turns out that in the early period debate about how Jesus ought to be understood was one of the greatest hindrances to unity. The first ecumenical council of the Christian church, led by the Roman Emperor Constantine (the Council of Nicaea in 325), in part suppressed certain ways of understanding Jesus. Constantine aimed at unifying his empire and that in part meant bringing unity in the church, particularly with respect to how Jesus was understood. An orthodox view was affirmed in the Creed of Nicaea. It did not succeed, however, in eliminating the diversity of views about Jesus; diversity survived, and in fact has continued to survive.

In the first-century canonical gospels, clearly Jesus was regarded as the divine Son of God, mythically portrayed as bigger than life. But oddly those words, as such, are never found as an admission on Jesus' own lips; the title "Son of God" is bestowed on him by others. And only once does Jesus accept the title Messiah ("Anointed"; Mark 14:61–62). In the passages parallel to Mark, he avoids such an admission. In Romans 1:3–4, a pre-Pauline confession or hymn, Jesus is not presented as divine, but as by nature essentially a human being, appointed or adopted by God for a special purpose. Others believed that Jesus was not human after all, but rather that he was completely divine, and only seemed to be human (cf. Phil 2:9–11 and John 1:1–2, 14). Jesus' humanity, including what he said and did, essentially disappeared in the later ecclesiastical creeds. The Apostles' Creed, for example, leaps from the birth of Jesus to his death, omitting what Jesus said and did. Still other groups regarded Jesus as a human being who came to be inhabited at his baptism by a divine spirit ("the Christ") or believed that he was the natural born son of Mary and Joseph, that is to say, a human being like the rest of us, except that he was better. Throughout the first and second centuries the historical man Jesus effectively became an originating principle for a variety of ways of understanding him and his role in faith.

Since the rise of the Enlightenment in the late seventeenth century, Western culture has been challenged by human reason, and the impact of reason on the physical sciences, medicine, and particularly religion has been dramatic. In the "Age of Reason," which the Enlightenment began, the Bible lost its dominant role in human culture as the authoritative Word of God, a text that had shaped human lives and national psyches. Under the influence of critical thinking and historical analysis, the Bible has been reduced to a mere record of only one quest for religious meaning, among many others. The earth is no longer seen as the center of the universe, as once was thought, or even the center of its galaxy; it is only one blue and white planet that circles the sun of a tiny solar system on the outer edge of the Milky Way in a universe of multiple galaxies, where every star in the night sky is a sun. Under the influence of the physical sciences, Christian Heaven and Hell can no longer be conceived as specific locations existing anywhere in the universe. In popular thought people had regarded them as locatable in space—Heaven was "up there" and Hell "down there." But like God and the devil, they no longer exist in the same way that human beings, the earth, and space exist—that is, they do not occupy common space and time. It is no longer reasonable to conceive of an ethereal spiritual realm parallel to cosmic existence, a different dimension, as it were, which is home to gods, demons, evil spirits, angels, etc. If so where would it be? Science has split the atom and "seen" into the tiny "world" of quantum mechanics, as well as seen to the edge of an expanding universe. And if God, spirits, demons, and angels do not share common space and time with human beings, how could they possibly be hurtful or helpful to human beings? In short, since the Enlightenment, traditional Christian faith is on the way to being recognized as only one more ancient superstition.

In an age when human reason shapes the human psyche, the very foundations of traditional Christian faith have been shattered, and perhaps the very foundations of any and all religious belief have been seriously undermined. The question is: Has religion of any and all varieties become obsolete? And that is the question this book aims to answer. Roger Ray writes with intense passion and a contagious sense of confidence that it is possible to be "spiritual" without having recourse to the traditional Christian anthropomorphic view of God and a divine Jesus who died on the cross for human sins, without viewing the world as inhabited by supernatural entities that either help or harm, and without fearing God may consign your immortal soul to Hell. For Ray, God is conceived as being present within everything that exists, but God is not to be identified with anything—God is something other than the cosmos and more than all existing things. He declines to quantify the "more" but argues that, in this way, persons of progressive faith can affirm the presence of the Divine in the cosmos and not use anthropomorphic terms. In progressive faith, Jesus is "a teacher of radical compassion and self-sacrificing devotion to the truth." He serves as "a symbol of the kind of spiritual depth" that persons of progressive faith must achieve "in order to transform the world."

Progressive faith expresses itself in a spiritual engagement with the world to bring about that transformation by: alleviating poverty and working in the trenches of government to realize justice in the social order, eliminating racism and prejudice wherever it surfaces, proclaiming an ecological message that protects the environment of the earth, and by working for peaceful solutions to issues that threaten the harmony of all societies.

His manifesto for progressive faith is forcefully and eloquently argued. Readers may disagree with some of his premises, but they will be deeply impressed by his sense of urgency and his absolute confidence that the superstition-based religions of the present and the past will have no meaningful role in the future of humanity.

One promising hope for the future, however, lies in a progressive faith, which will greatly facilitate the evolution of human culture towards a more just and compassionate society.

Charles W. Hedrick

Emeritus Professor of Religious Studies

Missouri State University

Acknowledgments

THIS SLIM VOLUME COMES into existence, in large part, due to the consistent encouragement, challenge, and occasional insistence of my friend Dr. Charles Hedrick, who has also devoted undeserved sacrificial time to helping me to put it all into final form. I also owe a personal thanks to my friend and parishioner Debbie Baugh, who both edited original drafts and continued to cheer me on towards the finish line. They have both devoted so much energy to reading various drafts of this work that I feel that their names should be on the cover of the book rather than just being given this acknowledgment here. I am sincerely very grateful to them both.

I also want to thank Colonel Ron Hertenstein for his editorial comments and challenges to my chapter on the ethics of modern warfare. Even where we do not agree, I find the Colonel's comments to be helpful and possibly even more reasonable than my own conclusions. In those places, however, I claim the right of the clergy to "call 'em like I see 'em."

Finally, and most importantly, I must thank the loving and faithful members of the Community Christian Church of Spring-field, Missouri, who have not only employed me and suffered through my prickly personality and approach to ministry but who have allowed me to literally experiment (hopefully more *with* them than *on* them) as we have tried to work out what it means to be a progressive faith community. It has been an ever-changing target but together we are striving to get this church business figured out.

Dr. Hedrick never tires of reminding me that I also owe thanks to my most vociferous critics who harassed me out of denominational ministry, freeing me to do the thinking and changing necessary to finally marry parish life to academic life in a congruent whole. I can be sincerely thankful for the outcome even if I cannot yet be thankful for the process. I wish for intellectual freedom for all members of the clergy but I hope that they manage to find it in a gentler path than the one I followed.

Introduction

To move forward in our practice, we seek to move from the intellect to faith. We grow from blind faith towards wisdom faith.[1]

RIDING ALONG A ROUGH dirt road through the jungles of Nicaragua near Matagalpa, my traveling companion explained to me that the farmer whose land we were crossing had lost his entire herd of cattle recently because a neighbor had left his well uncovered overnight, and a demon had come out and killed the cattle. Javier was not lying to me or trying to frighten me with ghost stories. He was telling me what he believed to be true, just as the Spanish priests who first came to Nicaragua to convert the natives had placed a cross by the opening of the nearby Masaya Volcano to keep Satan from emerging from its deep and smoky pit.

When I was a young teenager working on a neighbor's farm in the summer of 1969, the hay harvest was abysmal due to the dry weather we had that growing season in southern Kentucky. The farmer told me, literally with tears in his eyes, that those men had gone up to the moon the month before and done something that would change our weather so that it was never again going to rain in our area. Again, he was not a liar, nor was he insane. The farmer from my youth, like the priests of the Spanish conquistadors and my Nicaraguan friend, Javier, were describing the world as they understood it.

---

1. The Venerable Lama Migmar, speaking in Dr. Diana Eck's course on World Religions at Harvard in October 2004.

Religious dogma began in the same way. People tried to find the most plausible explanation they could for why some children do not survive, why normally life-giving rivers sometimes flood and wreak disasters, and why some years the harvest is great and some years winter brings the threat of starvation. At least according to their myths of origin, religious beliefs were the best and most plausible explanation for the things that happened in life. There was not a divide between science and religion because everyone was only interested in the truth. When that truth becomes an unchanging dogma that we are told to believe even when solid evidence points us in another direction, then that belief becomes a truth-denying religion that is inevitably harmful to its adherents and divisive in society.

It did rain on my neighbor's farm shortly after he had predicted that it would never rain again, and so that myth was never repeated. There is no way to prove a demon did not come out of an uncovered well in rural Nicaragua and kill a man's cattle, though there is probably a better explanation that has nothing to do with a well left carelessly uncovered overnight.

A couple of the books that almost made it into the Christian New Testament were written by Clement, a late first-century bishop in Rome. There are other reasons why these very popular letters of encouragement from Clement were not included in the final form of the New Testament, but at least one reason, which should have been reason enough, appears in chapter 25 of *1 Clement*. Clement confidently tells his readers that in Arabia there is a bird called a phoenix that lives for five hundred years:

> Let us take note of the remarkable and symbolic phenomenon encountered in the East, that is, in the vicinity of Arabia. For there is a bird which is called the phoenix. It is the only one of its kind and lives five hundred years. When the hour of its death approaches, it makes itself a nest out of frankincense and myrrh and other spices, and when its time has come it gets into and dies. Then as its flesh decays a kind of worm is produced which is nourished by the secretions of the carcass and grows wings. Then when it is grown it takes the nest containing

the bones of its predecessor and manages to carry them
all the way from Arabia to the Egyptian city called He-
liopolis. Whereupon in broad daylight, in plain sight of
everyone, it alights upon the altar of the sun and deposits
them there; and then starts back again. The priests then
consult their record of dates and find that it has come at
the end of the five-hundredth year.[2]

In the second century, when the canon of the New Testament was
in formation, even though the letters of Clement were widely read
and loved, someone likely had the sense to object, "You know,
this phoenix thing could make us all look pretty stupid." The early
church wanted to publish in their sacred text only what they were
certain was true.

Still, in our day, there are people who insist upon adherence
to ancient religious convictions that are just as clearly not true. The
Bible contains accounts of a talking snake, a talking donkey, a dis-
embodied floating hand that writes on the wall, a man who lived
in the stomach of a fish for three days, and prophet who raises
the dead, and there are also the accounts of Jesus raising the dead,
walking on water, and turning jars of water into delicious wine.

The current generation will no more believe that there is a
supernatural deity enthroned in the clouds who will send some
to heaven and many more to hell than you, my dear reader, were
inclined to believe that Neil Armstrong had messed up the moon
in some way that stopped rain from falling on Kentucky or that a
farmer in Javier's neighborhood had accidentally loosed a demon
out of his well one night. Telling people—even if you tell them
in a very big building adorned with stained glass and candles—to
believe in things for which there is neither evidence nor ability to
test the claims, will cease to work. Still, many of us believe that
there is a value to preserving a life of faith as we try to try to see the
world's events through a spiritual lens.

An "introduction" should help to usher readers into the
whole of the work in hand, and so a few definitions of words are
necessary, especially because the meaning of the words used in the

2. *1 Clem.* 25:1–5.

church environment are changing so rapidly. The older nomenclature that described religious people as being fundamentalist, evangelical, conservative, liberal, independent, liturgical, denominational, non-denominational, mainline, traditional, old-line, charismatic, Pentecostal, or holiness has lately been expanded to include the words *progressive* and *emerging* or *emergent*. I like and have used the term *emerging* because, to me, it references the kind of church that is emerging from the ashes of the rapidly failing forms of denominational and traditional Christianity. However, *emergent* is also a word used by a large group of neo-Pentecostals who practice faith healing, speak in tongues, and take notions of a supernatural theistic God very seriously. I have mistakenly attended conferences, retreats, and festivals that were advertised under the rubrics of "progressive" or "emerging" only to discover that their theology was consistent with conservative evangelical thinking, but they distinguished themselves from their roots in only one or two areas, such as hosting a beer garden at their events, demonstrating tolerance if not full acceptance of homosexuality, and I have seen evidence of a growing interest in social justice work.

I use the word *progressive* in a fairly concrete way. While many use the term as a kind of umbrella under which traditionalists and liberals can comfortably stand in a religious community that is accepting of both evangelical certainty and questioning uncertainty, that is not my meaning. For me, progressive faith is the long-awaited marriage of academic history, theology, biblical criticism, and comparative religion with congregational life. Therefore, while it is always preferable for everyone to be gracious about matters of personal faith and practice, I will not even feign indifference about choosing between critical thinking and magical thinking. The problem with most institutional religion is its baggage of magic and superstition and so my presentation of progressive faith will not, even for the sake of being polite, give the appearance of indifference on this front.

The purpose of this book is to embrace the synthesis of science with religion, the mind married to the heart, to try to articulate both an evidence-based faith and to apply that faith to life.

What we believe must also have a "therefore" that directs our path into reshaping the world for a new era. There never was a phoenix that arose from the remains of a previous incarnation, but there may be a new church emerging (there's that word again!) from the ruins of old denominations and mistaken religious doctrines. That's the church I'm looking for, and the one I will try to describe in this book.

1

Evidence-Based Faith

I wish to propose for the reader's favorable consideration a doctrine which may, I fear, appear wildly paradoxical and subversive. The doctrine in question is this: that it is undesirable to believe a proposition when there is no ground whatever for supposing it is true. I must of course admit that if such an opinion became common it would completely transform our social life and our political system.[1]

—BERTRAND RUSSELL

There is a new wave of reason sweeping across America, Britain, Europe, Australia, South America, the Middle East and Africa. There is a new wave of reason where superstition had a firm hold.[2]

—RICHARD DAWKINS

"THE ROOM IS FILLED with four foot tall Skrinchen," my philosophy professor asserted. "They are," Dr. Jim Spicer told his freshman students, "invisible and without mass and they are visible only to me." Dr. Spicer introduced me at the age of eighteen to the concept of an *a priori* truth claim that could not be verified by any external evidence nor be subjected to any sort of test. Though there was no way to prove that the room was not full of Skrinchen, there was also

1. Russell, *Sceptical Essays*, 1.
2. Quoted in Symphony of Science, "A Wave of Reason."

no particular reason to believe that he was telling the truth. Still, I knew that I would be foolish to believe that I was surrounded by these invisible beings. It would take me another decade to have the courage to apply this same conclusion to what I had been told by my Sunday school teachers about angels, demons, a talking snake, and so much more. After years of trying to teach philosophy and religion to my own college students, I recognize the difficulty in trying to explain how a story can convey important life principles while not being either literally or historically factual.

We believe much of what we believe because our family, community, church, or nation have passed along those beliefs, and we would be out of sync with our world if we did not also go along. In matters such as putting the fork on the left hand side of the plate, shaking hands with our right hands, or standing for the national anthem, it is just easier to go along than to demand a persuasive explanation. But when it comes to being told that, for example, being a homosexual is a sin worthy of eternal punishment, or that women cannot be leaders in faith communities, or that you must belong to one certain sect of one certain religion or risk becoming anathema to the Almighty Creator of the universe, then some critical thinking is called for.

The famous philosophical maxim known as Occam's Razor is often mistakenly used to imply that the simplest answer is likely to be the right answer. What Occam's Razor actually says is that the solution requiring the fewest number of unverifiable assumptions is the most likely answer.[3] So, if I ask you if the room is full of Skrinchen and you consider that there is no detectable evidence for the presence of Skrinchen except for some facetious philosophy professor who asks you to assume that he is telling you the truth, then the most obvious logical conclusion is that there are no Skrinchen present. While you could be wrong, there is no good reason to assume that you are not right.

This becomes rather more complex, however, when authority figures, your parents, and your friends and classmates are all fairly united in telling you that there are Skrinchen in the room.

3. Baker, "Simplicity."

Then you have to be more resolved in your application of critical thinking to avoid falling in line with the generally shared faith in Skrinchen.

Of course, belief or disbelief in the existence of Skrinchen does not affect how you will live. Assertions about heaven and hell, a final judgment, the nature of salvation, the definition of sin—these do matter. In fact, they may matter more than anything else in life and yet, for the most part, there is not much evidence to substantiate these supernatural claims, and attempts at giving evidence generally do not stand up to critical analysis.

A pastor I know told me about a friend of his who had visited a medium when he was a member of the Allied forces occupying Germany shortly after WWII. The medium had channeled the young soldier's deceased father. The spirit allegedly told the soldier about the existence of a half-brother, even revealing the sibling's name and address. The soldier contacted the man and discovered that what the spirit had told him through the medium was true. "How," my friend asked me, "can you explain that if there is no life after death?"

So I asked, "What did the medium tell him on his second visit?" "Well," he replied, "he never went back again." "Really," I asked, "for a few dollars he got to speak to his deceased father, discovered a previously unknown brother, and he never went back again?" I'm not saying that paranormal events never take place. I can no more say that there are no angels or demons than I can prove that there are no Skrinchen hiding behind every tree and rock, but if a truth claim is not repeatable or testable then we cannot rationally draw any conclusions from these reported angel sightings, ESP experiences, or visions. The events may be very powerful or even life-changing for the individual, but a private experience remains just that—private. Maybe they are accurately describing an event or maybe their memories become embellished in the retelling. As neurologists have reported in their research about memory, repeated retelling of a story often erases actual memories, and all that a person can remember is their elaborately embellished accounts. They are not lying about the memory; they are giving an honest account of their memory, but their memory itself has become a fictional account.[4]

This, of course, was the problem that Paul, the author and inspiration of much of the New Testament, faced when he sought to convert the people he encountered to the version of faith that was so important to him. He never met Jesus of Nazareth in the flesh; he had to rely on his visions. Only those who were willing to suspend critical thinking could fully accept what he had to say. He had no more evidence to offer that Jesus was raised from the dead than Clement, the popular first-century bishop of Rome, had for his insistence that the phoenix lived for five hundred years and then was reborn from the decayed remains.

Like Paul, Clement tried to add weight to his claim by saying that the newly born phoenix would carry the bones of the recently deceased phoenix to a temple in Egypt where priests recorded the arrival of the bird with the bones and nest of his predecessor on the five hundredth anniversary of the previous phoenix. Of course, there never was such a magical bird, but Clement had news of it from sources he trusted and—this may be the more important part—he believed it because he wanted to believe it.

If you want to believe that God wrote the Bible or that you have a literal soul that lives forever (even if trees, birds, and bees don't), then you can find reasons that support your belief—I prayed that it wouldn't rain on our picnic and it didn't rain . . . Thank you Jesus! . . . Too bad about all of those prayers for the end of the civil war in Syria. Perhaps God was too busy defending picnics from rain?

While it is impossible to be free of the prejudice of preference, still, we can strive to be as objective as possible in our application of critical thinking. One of the hazards faced by progressive religious people is that once we are set at liberty from the constraints of old creedal claims, some find themselves falling headlong into seemingly more attractive and less destructive truth claims that are just as dependent upon untestable assumptions as the religion from which they escaped.

4. Johnson, "Cognitive and Brain Mechanisms."

It was bad theology that led to the Crusades, to the divine right of kings, inquisitions, and sectarian religious wars, some of which were fought on battlefields, but many more divided families at the dinner table. There is good theology and there is bad theology. Critical thinking does matter. Sloppy thinking leads to uncertain results. Novices who have rejected the formal religion of their youth will often cobble together a more savory concoction that they will call Buddhism or Native American spirituality, much of which they made up last week after watching a really good movie, but—to call upon Occam's Razor once more—if they are trading one truckload of irrational assumptions for a new and more exotic-sounding truckload of irrational assumptions, the implications are likely to be equally unsavory.

Our preference for good manners, getting along well with others, and desire to avoid conflict, often lead us to a nearly sacramental love of false equivalents. I would invite anyone who says, "Everyone's religion is a private choice," or simply "To each his or her own," to take the time to visit their local shelter for victims of domestic violence or for teen "runaways." In my experience, a huge portion of the teen "runaway" population did not run away; they were kicked out of their family home because the religion of their parents kept them from accepting homosexuality, even if the homosexual in question was their own son or daughter. The misogyny that lies at the root of a great deal of domestic violence can be traced directly to the pulpits that influence the abusers. Mental health professionals have been trying to point out the connection between teen suicide and homophobic religious teachings for years.[5] Sloppy thinking doesn't just lead to unnecessary feelings of guilt and fear, but there is actually a casualty count and therefore, at the risk of alienating some for appearing to be impolite and lacking in diplomacy skills, I emphatically push for my peers in the religious world to be as rigorous in their scholarship and their critical thinking as is humanly possible.

The media has largely fallen prey in the past generation to a belief in false equivalents that compels them to appear to be

5. Freedman, "Gay Harassment."

neutral in almost every case, giving equal time to both sides of any issue. Sometimes the sides are just not equal. Note that when almost any television news outlet talks about global climate change, they will give almost equal time to those who deny climate change as they give to those who warn against the human behaviors causing climate change. Among climate scientists, there is more than a 90 percent consensus that it is our consumption of fossil fuels that is driving climate change.[6] It should also be noted that many of those denying climate change are on the payroll of the fossil fuel industries, and yet a false value placed on neutrality prevents the news media from communicating to the public important facts relevant to the survival of our race.[7] We can be thankful for civility in virtually every case, and yet the truth should not be sacrificed on the altar of being well behaved.

I am grateful for editors and friends who help me to see the other side of issues about which I may have allowed my own emotions or prejudices to lead me astray. Such calls for balance and objectivity are indispensable to any sincere scholar or pastor, but only insofar as they are encouraging the search for what is true, not when they are simply attempting to enforce either silence or the comfort of acquiescence to the *consensus mundi*.

For many in the religious community, "faith" has meant the ability to believe, as being true, that for which there is little or no evidence. When I would ask questions about what we had heard in church on the car ride home every Sunday, my mother would tell me, "You have to take it on faith." For her, the ability to make oneself believe totally irrational truth claims was a virtue to be acquired at all costs and every truly good person manages to do it. So I tried. I read the Bible over and over again. I majored in philosophy and religion in college, went to seminary, earned a doctorate in ministry and even did postdoctoral studies, and every step of the way my mother's injunction to "just take it on faith," became increasingly impossible.

6. NASA, "Consensus: 97%."
7. Green Peace, "Koch Industries."

I no longer associate the word "faith" with the willful assassination of my brains. I am grateful to Karen Armstrong and Marcus Borg for recovering an older and more meaningful interpretation of faith to mean something more akin to courage or commitment. And so I invite you, my readers, to have courage as we rethink what it means to be a person of faith in the twenty-first century. No longer will we accept the demand of fealty to creeds and doctrines that do not describe the reality of the world we experience. Our religion will be a religion that allows for a spiritual perspective on what is demonstrably true.

2

What Do Progressives Mean When We Say "God"?

For "In him we live and move and have our being"; as even some of your own poets have said, "For we too are his offspring." Since we are God's offspring, we ought not to think that the deity is like gold, or silver, or stone, an image formed by the art and imagination of mortals. (Acts 17:28–29)

LONG BEFORE OUR ANCESTORS had either organized religion or organized speech they became aware of their existence and their mortality. The anxiety produced by the knowledge that they would die provoked the original humans' search for meaning in existence. Before we pretended to understand how the leaves on trees turn sunlight into sugar or how the collision of a cold front with a warm front spawns tornadoes, many things in life provoked wonder. We moderns occasionally need to be reminded that there is a huge difference between being able to describe an event and actually understanding that event. While people in earlier times believed that God held the planets in their orbits around the sun, the mere fact that we can describe the complexities of certain properties of physics does not mean that we understand how they work.

To premodern humans, simply looking up at the night sky, or the awareness that summer will always follow winter just as the sun will always "rise" again, demanded an explanation. In primitive cultures, the sun itself was a divine figure, as was the earth. For them, the wind was not the result of solar heating of distant oceans but rather the breath of an invisible deity. Most commonly, we experience and respond to life through our emotions and so it was natural to assume that when the rain didn't come, or the rivers flooded, or the winter was too harsh the gods were angry, offended, or awaiting some sacrifice or devotion.

We initially conceived of gods in our own image. Like us and like nature itself, our gods were capricious, sometimes loving and generous, sometimes jealous and vindictive. We talked of gods who were like us, only bigger, stronger, and with longer lives but with all of the foibles and appetites we experience. So we built houses for our gods to live in. We sacrificed food on altars to feed them, poured out wine and blood to appease them, sang songs to praise them, and endured tedious rituals to satisfy their narcissistic need for attention.

But even from the dawn of civilization there were always those who felt that we were selling the Divine Other short by trying to turn God or gods into men and women. According to the writer of Acts, the apostle Paul, attempting to connect with a Greek audience in Athens, quoted a poet-philosopher, Epimenides, from more than five hundred years earlier, who said that Zeus was not dead but was instead ever living and that "in him, we live and move and have our being."

Somehow there have always been some among us who could see that no religion defines God; no idol, painting, stained glass window, or statue could meaningfully describe God. Yet we always feel compelled to try to express our profound existential experiences in concrete language. One of my theology professors used to call this "trying to eff the ineffable."

We cannot avoid speaking of our lives in the language that is based in experience. Consider the difference in the way that Paul describes his mystical experience and the way a later generation described it for him, after Paul was long dead. In his own words, Paul says,

> I know a person in Christ who fourteen years ago was
> caught up to the third heaven—whether in the body or
> out of the body I do not know; God knows. And I know
> that such a person—whether in the body or out of the
> body I do not know; God knows—was caught up into
> Paradise and heard things that are not to be told, that no
> mortal is permitted to repeat. (2 Cor 12:2–4)

You see, Paul gives us no concrete visuals. He knows that
something profound happened to him but he resolutely avoids using language about winged angels or a giant enthroned divine king.
If you were an artist or an illustrator, how would you portray this
experience? How could a movie capture what Paul is describing?

A generation later, Luke, writing the book of Acts to bolster
Paul's reputation, describes what I am suggesting was the same experience in this way in Acts (and in slightly different forms twice
more in Acts 22 and 26):

> Now as he was going along and approaching Damascus,
> suddenly a light from heaven flashed around him. He
> fell to the ground and heard a voice saying to him, "Saul,
> Saul, why do you persecute me?" He asked, "Who are
> you, Lord?" The reply came, "I am Jesus, whom you are
> persecuting. But get up and enter the city, and you will
> be told what you are to do." The men who were travel-
> ling with him stood speechless because they heard the
> voice but saw no one. Saul got up from the ground, and
> though his eyes were open, he could see nothing; so they
> led him by the hand and brought him into Damascus.
> For three days he was without sight, and neither ate nor
> drank. (Acts 9:3–9)

Luke, the presumed author of Acts,[1] takes an indescribable
experience and turns it into a visually rich narrative that has inspired museums full of paintings and that has appeared in countless

---

1. Though no clear consensus among biblical scholars exists, because the
letters of Paul precede the writing of the canonical gospels and Acts, I come
down on the side of believing that the gospel writers were generally aware of
the letters and theology of Paul. Paul's evolved Christology seems to be echoed
in the gospel tradition in ways that support this assumption.

movies. Luke turns Paul's ineffable experience into a very concrete experience but an experience about which Paul never said anything. And, in my understanding of Paul's character, if Paul did have an experience like this he would never have stopped talking about it! But it is much the same for most of us. We have a deeply felt experience of a divine presence but talking about that experience is like trying to nail smoke to the wall. Anything we say starts to limit the experience and to diminish its value.

Luke wanted his readers to be persuaded that Paul was God's chosen messenger and so he adds details intended to be persuasive that, in the light of critical analysis, will likely seem absurd. Our Sunday school teachers may have tried to persuade us that there was a time in antiquity when such things happened with regularity but that they simply do not happen now. How is that true? Did God go into retirement? Did God just enjoy hanging out in first-century Palestine but twenty-first century America is not inviting? Did the Divine intervene in human history in visible and miraculous ways twenty centuries ago but for some unknown reason just stopped mixing it up with humans? Or is it simply that the ancients expressed their experiences in terms that we must translate into the language that reflects our current realities? Again, I will mention the application of Occam's Razor: that the most likely reality is the one that will require the fewest number of unsubstantiated assumptions.

When I started graduate school more than three decades ago, our professors were trying to teach us to stop referencing God as being male, and just that obvious move from seeing God as a Caucasian, white-haired and bearded giant in the clouds met with angry resistance. It isn't until you say, "Oh, God is a man? How big are his feet? How long is his beard?" will people begin to give up on the concrete image of God as a person. To be male rather than female implies the presence of boy parts and trying to describe those divine parts is a conversation stopper in most Sunday school classes. Some things only become obvious when pushed to absurdity.

Hopefully the matter of God having a gender is long settled, but the problem of our desire for concrete images in which to conceive of God persists. We use images to try to express ourselves, to understand and to communicate our experiences.

When we were young, our first science teachers showed us illustrations of atoms with little colored balls called neutrons and protons and they were surrounded by brightly glowing electrons moving in predictable orbits in assigned shells around the nucleus of the atom. In our young minds, actual atoms, if we could see them, would have looked just like this.

Of course, you cannot see an atom, and if you could it would look nothing like the model, yet the model helped us to understand atoms, their behavior and nature, and so models helped us to form a basis for talking about chemistry, biology, and physics. In fact, we would likely never have made much progress in our comprehension of science if we had not, at the beginning, oversimplified reality just to get a toehold on the initial climb up into the light of understanding.

Similarly, we began our religious education with stories about miracles, making tablets out of modeling clay to look like the Ten Commandments and learning about anthropomorphic images of the God who defies description. We imagined God in human form. We created a God who feels what we feel, who understands us, and yet loves us.

The dark shadows of our minds sought to resolve our feelings of guilt and fear by creating an imagined pathway out of mortality and death and into a state of forgiveness, acceptance, and even of eternal reward. Not all religions have a clear concept of an afterlife, but the experience of the weak and abused filled them with a longing for some universal justice, some way to balance the scales of life. A final judgment followed by either reward or punishment gave the poor and enslaved, the victims of abuses of power, the opportunity to believe that a loving God would eventually punish their oppressors and bless them, the righteous and deserving, with a glorious reward.

Many still find faith in such a final reward and punishment in eternity so crucial to their ability to cope with the injustice of life that they are committed to religious bodies and creeds that reassure them that heaven and hell, these ideas that began in the imagination of ancient Persian slaves, are literally true.[2]

Millions are willing to suspend critical thinking to accept as evidence accounts of near-death experiences of "going towards the light," seeing long-dead friends and relatives, and being drawn back into their earthly bodies by some medical miracle that evidently came as a surprise to their supernatural theistic image of God. The recent popularity of Eben Alexander's book *Proof of Heaven* speaks to the desperation many feel for certainty. Alexander is a neurosurgeon and so he seems to speak with the kind of credibility and authority the ancients once bestowed upon their high priests. Ironically, though the word "proof" is in the title of the book, no critically satisfying proof is offered anywhere in the book.

I am unapologetically dismissive of such thinly veiled attempts at confounding readers untutored in medical jargon to give undeserved credibility to personal accounts rendered in seemingly scientific language. I read these accounts in much the way you might hear a primitive describing a flashlight as a magical stick that has captured the sun. That so many allow themselves to be persuaded by such obvious self-delusion is testimony to how desperate we are for some hope for eternity and for justice.

Still, while we must graciously allow everyone the freedom to believe and practice as they wish as long as they do no harm to others, those of us who strive to embrace an evidence-based faith should open our minds to new ways of trying to articulate a less anthropomorphic view of the divine. Bowing to the objective truth of the sciences should not remove the existential experience of awe, wonder, and even marvel at the universe. Mystery is not the same thing as myth or magic. We can reject superstitious thinking while

2. Conceptions of life after death vary broadly in antiquity. I am here giving credit to the Persian Zoroastrian religion for giving Judaism, Christianity, and Islam, as well as other popular religions that are no longer with us, the basic construct of a place of eternal punishment and a place of eternal reward that all people must face.

embracing the profundity of a real universe that ultimately defies comprehension and continually astonishes us to the core of our being with beauty, paradox, and wonder at both the grand scale of the universe and the remarkable art, geometry, color, and diversity in a microscopic view of something as common as a pinch of sand or a drop of pond water.

Many of the scholars most dear to progressive religious thinkers call themselves *panentheists*. The term may be new to many modern religious people but the concept is as old as Epimenides, who conceived of God as something other than a person with a body who was "out there" somewhere. The ancient Hebrews resisted creating statues or images of God because God, as a spirit, could only be diminished by trying to describe the Divine in human terms.

Western religious people often look at the religions of the East such as Buddhism or Confucianism and wonder aloud if they are really religions because they lack a single supernatural theistic God or a clear view of heaven and hell. Hinduism, with its many gods, is even more confusing to those who *ipso facto* assume that monotheism is superior to polytheism.

Eastern religions were not captured by the push towards the attempts at monotheism we see in Judaism, Christianity, and Islam. But, to be honest, no monotheism has ever succeeded in staying the course; they have found it necessary to add other virtual "gods" in the form of demons and spirits to account for the bad things in life. Popular monotheistic religions could not resist creating semi-divine characters, such as in the incarnation of God in Jesus or the saints to whom Catholics pray for special blessings, or the angels and demons of Muslim and Jewish lore. Any attempt at describing the Christian Trinity as an expression of monotheism requires verbal gymnastic arguments worthy of an Olympic gold medal, but Trinitarian views cannot realistically be monotheistic.

Much of the attraction in recent years to the Buddhist view of the Divine is specifically because of its lack of specificity. Buddhists teach that all that exists is connected and the Divine is united with the all. As the ancient poet said, we all live and move and have our being in God. God is not a rock or a tree, but all rocks and trees are in God. God is not "out there" only but is both "out there" and "in here." There are, of course, many forms of Buddhism and some will include more talk about the devas, non-human spirits, but it is safe to understand such things as being personifications of either things or ideas and not actual invisible, floating spirits.

The fact that Buddhists refrain from trying to describe God does not mean that they do not believe in a divine presence. That Hindus express their understanding of the Divine in hundreds of god-like images is just another way of being open to a multiplicity of existential experiences of the Divine. It is likely the most accurate way to understand the pantheon of Hindu gods is as personifications of what we experience in life.

In fact, a persuasive case can be made for laying the blame for most religious wars at the doorstep of monotheism. If you have a concrete worldview that says, "My religion is not only right, but is so very, very right that anyone who disagrees with my religion is evil and possibly even deserving of being destroyed for blasphemy," then you have the historical basis for many tragic human conflicts.

Most wars can best be understood by the old adage, "Follow the money." Kings and presidents use high-sounding moral or religious reasons for going to war but usually it is about power, real estate, or capital wealth. Even if the motivations of governments likely had little or nothing to do with religious beliefs, the hearts of believers left them vulnerable to being recruited to crusades and wars in the name of an indefensible theology.

Paul Tillich, the twentieth-century theologian, created a great deal of public controversy when he said, "God does not exist. He is being itself beyond essence and existence. Therefore to argue that God exists is to deny him."[3] Though many chose to interpret that as a statement of atheism, what he was saying, in a very intentionally provocative way, was that God does not have a body or a place, is not a thing or a person, and in that sense does not exist within

---

3. Tillich, *Systematic Theology*, 205.

time and space. Tillich was not an atheist. He was what we now more commonly call a panentheist.[4]

Pantheism is the belief that the universe is God, but panentheism differentiates itself from pantheism in that, though the universe is in God, the sum total of rocks, trees, planets, and stars is not itself God. God is all of that and something more. And yet, almost anything we say past that starts to look like trying to nail smoke to the wall. Use every nail in your carpenter's belt and you will still have accomplished nothing and maybe will have done a lot of damage to a perfectly good wall. As Tillich said, God is the ground of our being, although trying to turn that profound awareness into a person by attributing anthropomorphic emotions, will, intent, or even intervention in human history, is bound to end up in error. As one who lives and moves and has his being in God, I prefer to speak not so much in piled up adjectives about God but in terms of how my awareness of God gives me a spiritual perspective on life. A strict humanist, an Epicurean, or a libertarian may seek either exclusively or primarily to scratch his or her own itches, to desire her or his own comfort and joy. Those who affirm that there is a vital connection between all persons and the universe itself are more likely to choose to strive to honor that connection to all other people and to the earth in ways that provide the greatest good to the largest number of people and to the planet itself. That is not a natural or a necessary choice. It is a conscious choice to embrace this kind of spirituality, this perspective on reality.

A panentheist's spirituality may express itself in forms of community ritual or in choosing to avoid goods manufactured by slaves or forms of transportation that accelerate the pollution of the planet. I will say much more about the implications of a spiritual worldview in the final portion of this work, but for now I am inviting you to let go of all idolatry, all anthropomorphic images of God.

Panentheism then, for me, becomes the most effective way of bringing both scientific inquiry and spiritual concerns together into a consistent synthesis. It also allows for a greater interfaith

4. Cooper, *Panentheism*, 24.

cooperation. There is an excellent introduction to panentheism in Marcus Borg's book *Speaking Christian*,[5] though it is the assumed theology of such authors as Bishop John Shelby Spong, Rosemary Ruether, and Sally McFague and many more. But we also see it in Catholic scholars such as Martin Heidegger, Karl Rahner, and Hans Kung. We see panentheistic assumptions in the Hasidic Jewish scholar Martin Buber, the Sufi Muslim writer Muhammed Iqbal, and Buddhists such as Alan Watts and Massao Abe.

In poetic terms, Hal Taussig, in an essay entitled "Disparate Presence," speaks of meditating on a poem, a song, a leaf, a flower, the sunlight on the wall, fully anticipating each to have an impact on how he thinks, feels and acts. He says, "One might say that I treat these various objects before me as God. I would not disagree, but would hasten also to clarify. I do not conceive a collective consciousness behind these particulars. There is no ensemble making up a single whole."[6] In this sense, we can affirm the presence of the Divine without trying to cast a God in anthropomorphic terms, making the Divine into a person.

In the hope of preserving credible, meaningful, and relevant faith in the twenty-first century, let's stop trying to limit God to our own religion, stop trying to manipulate the Divine into doing our bidding, punishing our enemies or rewarding our friends. Let's take our foot off of God's throat, because, you know, God doesn't have a throat, and we look pretty silly trying to hold the Spirit down.

5. Borg, *Speaking Christian*, 73.

6. Hedrick, *When Faith Meets Reason*, 150.

3

What is Scripture to Progressives?

The Bible is not literal history; it is not eyewitness reporting. It is a Jewish book, written by Jewish authors, telling a profoundly Jewish story about an indefinable God working in a special human life. If we recover the Jewishness of the Bible, we will be freed from both the killing fundamentalism of our time and from the rebellion against that fundamentalism that masquerades as an unbelieving 'secular humanism.[1]

—BISHOP JOHN SHELBY SPONG

WOODY ALLEN ONCE SAID that he grew up in such a rough neighborhood that his mother actually made a good luck charm for him out of a rifle shell. He wore the bullet on a chain around his neck under his shirt to give him courage when facing the bullies in the neighborhood but it so happened that the bullet actually ended up saving his life. A crazed Gideon once threw a New Testament right at him and it would have gone right through his heart but the bullet under his shirt stopped it.

Those of us who grew up in those primitive times when the Gideons were allowed to come into public schools and make presentations to students are all too familiar with the stories of soldiers in WWII, Korea, and Vietnam who had kept a Gideon New Testament in their pocket and when they were shot, the bullet

1. Spong, "Part IV Matthew."

pierced the pages of the little Bible and stopped like a molten lead finger pointing at Psalm 91, "A thousand shall fall at thy side, and ten thousand at thy right hand; but it shall not come nigh thee" (91:7 KJV).The Christian Bible was presented to us as having uniquely divine properties. In Jewish faith communities, the Torah was to be copied by hand and, once blessed for use in the synagogue, it was never to be touched by human hands again. The text became sacred and was read publicly by lectors who followed along the ancient Hebrew with a golden pointer. In the event of a fire, or military attack, people risked their lives to rescue the Torah.

Among Muslims, the Quran is of such sacred importance that it was considered to be torture when American captors would throw a copy in the toilet or urinate on it in Guantanamo.[2] An idiotic, xenophobic preacher in Florida could almost start a war by threatening to burn copies of the Quran.

Christians have not historically been too far off from this level of devotion. Many of us can remember the day when it was common for families to display a huge open copy of the King James Bible in their living room, usually sitting on a hand-carved olive wood stand from Israel. Laws formerly existed in many states against defiling the Bible or even against putting any other book on top of a Bible.

The first little New Testament and Psalms I was given when I was eleven years old, I was told, could stop a bullet. Even as biblical scholarship has shone the light of reason on this ancient text, in some liturgical churches the Bible is still carried into their solemn assemblies accompanied by incense and a processional cross. Some communities stand when the Gospel is read aloud and reply "Thanks be to God" when they are liturgically informed that it is, in very fact, "the Word of the Lord."

But the solemn and sacred role of Scripture in society has been under attack. In recent years, as racism, anti-Semitism, misogyny, and homophobia have become socially unacceptable, the faithful have been compelled to play down or explain away the portions of the Bible that are clearly racist, anti-Semitic, misogynistic, and

2. BBC News, "US Guantanamo."

homophobic. What churches from fundamentalist and Pentecostal conservatives to liberal mainstream denominations have been afraid to say publicly is that they simply disagree with portions of the Bible.

Maybe there was a period of time when reproduction was so vital to the survival of ancient tribes that homosexual relationships were discouraged in order to promote propagation. Perhaps in primitive agrarian societies there were reasons for patriarchal control of land and even for slavery, but these attempts at whitewashing the abuses of the past because they were either economically necessary or culturally expedient are, at best, embarrassing.

When we read the Bible honestly, we see, for example, that both creation accounts in chapters 1 and 2 of Genesis describe the creation of a flat earth. The truth is that the earth is not flat. While there are things of value to be found in those ancient and poetic accounts of creation, scientific facts are not to be found there. In the real world, there are no talking snakes. Women were not made from one side[3] of a dirt-constructed man. There is no magical Garden of Eden guarded by a flaming sword and powerful angel to prevent humans from returning to it.

It was always a mistake to turn to the Bible for information about science, anthropology, history, or astronomy. It has been a cultural resource of poetry, music, morality plays, and ethical instruction and even though its authorship has been attributed to God, or to Spirit-inspired mortals, it is not even a collection of the best poetry, music, morality plays, or ethical instruction that we have from the same era. One need only read the works of Plato and Aristotle from the fourth century BCE to see how biblical literature of the same period and later pales in comparison. Still, the Bible contains beautiful images of social justice and advocacy for the poor, the sick, and the vulnerable, but we must acknowledge that it also has its passages of undeserved homage to royalty and priests. It does, in parts, treat women as if they were property or

3. There is no word in Hebrew for "rib." The Genesis narrative describes a side of the first person being taken. Perhaps we are invited to think of the first person being split into two halves, one becoming male and the other female.

livestock, and it disparages not only homosexuality but even some aspects of simply being a sexual human being.

Many scholars have for years tried to educate the literate public to a more sober view of the Bible as a collection of differing views of various peoples who lived over many different centuries, and none of whom, as comedian Bill Maher likes to point out, had any idea where the sun goes at night. Some of it is stunningly insightful, but some of it is horrifyingly evil. The same book that tells us to "Love your enemies, do good to those who hate you" (Luke 6:27) also praises Jephthah for murdering his own daughter to fulfill a battlefield vow (Judg 11:25–35). We would be crazy to try to read every part as having equal value for all time.

Some, such as the popular writer and thinker Michael Dowd, have suggested that it is time to simply set these ancient texts aside and to focus on the facts of our scientific age as our new scripture. Those of us who have spent our lives in the formal study of Scripture hear that statement with all of the enthusiasm with which the wagon builders heard the sound of the first Model A Ford coming down the road.

We have studied ancient languages, pored over ancient texts, and devoted ourselves to years of challenging and complicated biblical studies to become experts on a topic that may soon leave us looking like the last nerd with a slide rule in a leather holster on our belts. Already the Bible has the approximate value of a rotary phone to most people in Europe and the United States. Most people can remember when they had one, and they have nostalgic feelings about it, but if you gave them one today, they would have no use for it beyond decoration.

I still find the Bible to be endlessly interesting and I cannot even resist ordering the next new book produced by any of my favorite scholars. I even find the Revised Common Lectionary to be a helpful tool that I use as a personal discipline to force me to consider the preaching topics raised by this three-year cycle of prescribed Scripture lessons. Still, I no longer see Scripture as an authoritative voice in my life or in the church, but I find it to be helpful, in part because it is so familiar to our generation.

One only needs to say the name "Noah" and a story comes alive in the minds of those who grew up in church. A preacher can mention David and Bathsheba and suddenly the preacher and the congregation have a shared story between them. The passion narrative in the Gospels is an archetypal story. Who can hear the name "Judas" and not remember a former friend who has betrayed you? Who does not know what it is to have your closest family and friends stand in the distance watching you suffer through your darkest hour without saying a word?

Our generation will never have an entirely dispassionate relationship with Scripture, and we will continue to use it as our common ground for study, instruction, and in our rituals, in both weddings and funerals, on holidays, and even most Sundays. But this will not always be true. Inevitably, the generations that will follow us will not spend hours and hours of their growing up years studying and memorizing Bible passages, and those who will be the pastors of future faith communities will not likely feel the need to be immersed in biblical studies. Sadly, however, there is no clearly shared set of documents that will provide the common resources where we will meet in the future to discuss issues of lasting importance.

As recently as the late 1970s, among Protestant churches Sunday school attendance was approximately the same as the worship service attendance. By the end of the 1980s, that ratio had changed, with Sunday school attendance falling by more than half. Many mainstream churches have given up and no longer offer religious education at all because they simply do not know what to teach, and their members will no longer attend traditional classes.

The Center for Progressive Christianity is to be applauded for making a serious effort at writing ethical religious education materials for use in progressive churches. It remains to be seen whether or not progressive-leaning parents will make it a priority to expose their children to this education. We must first overcome the negative associations we have with past experiences of misinformation, possibly neurotic religious guilt, and an anti-intellectual worldview in order to make giving a more healthy religious education an important part of child rearing. At this juncture, we probably know more about what we don't want to pass along than we know with certainty what we do want to preserve for the generations to come.

Progressives make the conscious choice to abandon false certainty in favor of honest uncertainty. For us, the only scripture that matters is the truth, wherever we can find it. We will sometimes find our truth in science, sometimes in philosophy, and sometimes in a popular song or even a bumper sticker. As we throw our arms open to the whole world in a search for meaning, insight, and honesty, we no longer have a single book that will call scholars and sages to a common place where they can debate and evaluate a shared body of literature. We are losing something as the Quran, Torah, and Bible lose status in the minds of modern people of faith, but we also gain a new and exciting liberty to find a new way of living, unchained from loyalty to ancient texts that have inspired many of our highest ideals but also have polluted our lives with irrational prejudices and neurotic guilt.

We once enjoyed a certain stability in being able to say authoritatively, "The Bible says so!," but to be honest that injunction has not worked well for a long time for most of the world, if in fact it ever did. I cannot think of a time in history when it was common for people to sell all they owned and give it to the poor (Luke 18:22) nor even to predictably forgive someone seventy times seven times (Matt 18:22). We have always had a rather cafeteria-style approach to Scripture, and we have not usually even chosen the more important passages to take home with us after church was over.

Our generation is turning to our faith with less confident certainty but with new liberty to focus on truths that are more substantial. We will serve more meals in homeless shelters than we will serve Communion in our sanctuary. We will dig more wells for safe water for the poor in Nicaragua and Haiti than we will baptize people in solemn rituals. We will not speak confidently of a heaven in the afterlife, but we will fight with determination against the hell that is all too familiar in this world for those who live in poverty, who are refugees of wars, and who live in the pollution of an economic system that trades our only viable planet for current profit.

Setting aside ancient magic and superstition is not destroying the church. The church is being set free.

4

Which Jesus Do We Hold Most Dear?

Extraordinary claims require extraordinary evidence.[1]

—CARL SAGAN

NOT VERY MANY YEARS go by without a new popular book about Jesus dominating the market. Some are better than others, and though each would seem to have some redeeming qualities, none, it is fair to say, is either perfect or will prove to be the last word on the topic. Reza Aslan received a lot of media attention in the spring and summer of 2013 following the release of his book *Zealot*. Though Aslan now self-identifies as a Muslim, and he certainly gained a lot of notoriety for his publication of the history of Islam in *No God but God*, he presents in *Zealot* a fairly devotional, though non-divine view of the historical Jesus. In some ways, progressive Christians will find a natural ally in Muslim thinkers who affirmed more than a millennia ago that Jesus was a prophet but who consider it blasphemous to call him God. Still, we will not find many practicing Muslims who do not try to work Jesus into being a prophet of a supernatural theistic God. Even so, there should be some common ground for conversation between progressive Christians and Muslim scholars in the mutual affirmation

1. Sagan, "Encyclopaedia Galactica."

that no human is divine in a way that is different in kind from that way that all of us have a share in what we call "the Divine."

While the popularity of *Zealot* gave Aslan a forum to quote New Testament gospel passages as if they were reliable reports of what Jesus actually said, there are those on the other end of the spectrum who are attempting to support the claim that Jesus never existed. They say that there wasn't even a village named Nazareth in first-century Palestine and that the entire Jesus narrative was made up by second-century Roman aristocrats to create a religion that would calm down the peasants.[2]

We cannot realistically just brush the skeptics aside. There is not much in the written historical record about Jesus, and there is no physical evidence at all. Tourism is big business in Israel, so modern Christian pilgrims will be given tour guide assurances of exactly what they came to the "Holy Land" to find. Travelers to modern-day Jericho may be shown a sycamore tree that tour guides will tell them is the actual tree that Zacchaeus climbed in the gospel account of the encounter between Zacchaeus and Jesus (Luke 19). Etchings in the pavement in Jerusalem or even an old building dubbed the "Upper Room" are used to thrill tourists with the prospect of walking where Jesus walked or drawing near to historical evidence of gospel accounts. For more on this, I can only refer you to the proverb mistakenly attributed to P. T. Barnum: "There is a sucker born every minute."[3] But most of us have, at one time or another, fallen prey to being suckers for a good Jesus story because we so wanted to believe that what our pastors, priests, Sunday school teachers, parents, and peers had told us was true.

Though it seems most likely that there was a village known as Nazareth that was a poor Jewish suburb of Sephoris, a much larger city of blended Greek and Palestinian people, it is impossible to prove from currently extant written records and archaeological evidence is sketchy. I am disinclined to jump off the cliff with the skeptics and say that Jesus is a literary creation, but honesty

2. Humphres, "The Town That Theology Built."

3. Most people agree that the quote is most properly assigned to a contemporary and critic of P. T. Barnum, David Hannum.

compels us to acknowledge that most of the Jesus narrative is a matter of conjecture, tradition, and false attribution. More than a century of sincere and scholarly research into the historical Jesus has resulted in several quite plausible images of this Palestinian religious figure—and some scholars would even object to the idea that he was religious, not the least of which is the broadly published scholar Charles Hedrick. Hedrick sums his views up in an email written to me on April 13, 2014: "It is certainly clear that the historical man Jesus was not traditionally religious when compared to the Judean state religion centered in the temple at Jerusalem—even the synoptic gospels read traditionally make that clear. But when one considers the critical residue of his sayings, he appears to be rather secular in his outlook, and does not seem very religious in terms of either ancient or modern organized religions. He would, for example, have a difficult time being comfortable in contemporary Christian worship."

Most of what we know about Jesus we know from the four gospels in the New Testament, all of which were written to accomplish theological goals and none of which gives us eye witness or contemporary reports. Actually, our best support for the claim that Jesus even existed comes from the hand of the self-appointed apostle Paul. Paul never met Jesus and did not seem to have much interest in the actual history of Jesus the person. However, Paul does report having gone to Jerusalem and met with the family and close friends of Jesus with whom Paul was, essentially, a competitor. By his own reporting, his relationship with them was more than a little strained, and he was at considerable pains to make it clear that he didn't learn anything from them and was not indebted to those who actually knew Jesus for any part of what Paul preached (Gal 2:6: "And from those who were supposed to be acknowledged leaders [what they actually were makes no difference to me; God shows no partiality]—those leaders contributed nothing to me"). We could wish that he was a lot more curious and a lot less arrogant, but we have to depend on the Paul we have and not the Paul we might wish for.

It is not a stretch to say that were it not for Paul most of us would never have heard of Jesus. The Jesus tradition may have been just a brief blip on the radar of history had Paul not taken Jesus' name and sketchy historical background to use as the language set for the mystery religion Paul taught (a synthesis of Jewish thought with Greek salvation and other mystery religions). What we can say with confidence is that the message that was central to Paul and the message that was central to Jesus have little or nothing to do with one another.

It is evident that Jesus had a following that included at least one of his brothers, and all of us who have brothers can testify to the fact that this was no small feat. What Jesus said and did was sufficiently profound and meaningful to cause a following to remain intact after he was dead. So there were those who repeated what he said and told stories about what he did, but those traditions come down to us only through the four gospels of the New Testament and obscure non-canonical sources such as the fragmentary sayings sources, including the Gospel of Thomas and a few other pieces of gnostic writings.

Paul, as the first and most popular writer in the Christian tradition, undoubtedly influenced how all four canonical gospels were written. Mark is generally thought to be the oldest of the four gospels and the others were largely dependent on Mark's story line. Thirty years after the facts, Mark tells a martyr's tale beautifully, memorably, and persuasively. Matthew and Luke, written about twenty years later, add to the theological evolution of the Jesus tradition, and when another generation had passed at the end of the first century, the gospel attributed to John takes the final step in the evolution of Jesus being portrayed, literally, as God.

Paul, the first known author to write about the resurrection of Jesus, describes the event in 1 Corinthians 15 as a visionary event in which his own encounter with the resurrected Jesus was just like the experiences of Peter, James, John, and the other Jerusalem witnesses. Paul never mentions an empty tomb and would not likely have believed that the body of Jesus of Nazareth had been transformed into the spiritual Christ of Paul's theology. Mark's gospel gives us an empty tomb narrative but not a resurrection appearance. Matthew and Luke add resurrection appearances that are highly symbolic but do not agree with one another. John adds to the resurrection appearance traditions in even higher christological terms, which makes John the favorite of those who want a very divine Jesus. Traditional Christianity has tended to view all of the gospels through the lens of our least credible ancient witness, John. If we know almost nothing about the historical Jesus and if most progressives acknowledge that there is no incarnation, substitutionary death, or creedal path into a glorious afterlife, why is Jesus still important to us? The unsettling but honest answer is that Jesus is only important to us if we choose to gift him with importance. There is no supernatural theistic deity demanding a blood sacrifice to save us from eternal damnation. Progressives then see Jesus as being one of the many historical characters in whose name a body of spiritual teachings has been collected. We know the names of many others, and there are thousands more who have contributed to human spiritual evolution whose names are lost to history. Christianity has been historically and numerically successful for political and sociological reasons as much as for the actual content of the teachings of Jesus of Nazareth. Liberated from a controlling ecclesiastical authority and the darkness of premodern superstitions, we recognize that what draws us to a spiritual life is a desire for truth, meaning, and insight. Now the guiding issue is: Does the Jesus tradition have something to offer to the twenty-first century, and if it does, just what is that?

Of the major academic trends in historical Jesus studies, several paths do not lead us to a Jesus who offers much to us. If Jesus was only a reformer of first-century Judaism then, while he may have some historical interest to us, we would never be inclined to quote him as a moral authority in our lives. Even those who try to temper theological excesses with more realistic historical boundaries often end up trying to preserve a certain fealty to the institutional church's need for a supernatural God who intervenes in human history. I appreciate the helpful steps offered to the evolution of progressive faith by those authors who helped to build a bridge from traditional Christianity to a more progressive faith, but I cannot convince myself that there is a future for a Christianity that asks postmodern thinkers to accept the unverifiable truth claims of traditional orthodoxy.

"Extraordinary claims," as Carl Sagan has said, "demand extraordinary evidence," and no credible evidence exists for heaven, hell, a Trinity, souls, angels, demons, or a personal anthropomorphic God who is "out there" somewhere. The gospels, written long after Jesus' death by people who had never met him, record accounts of miraculous events from changing water into wine to restoring life to the dead, but we have no concrete reason to take any of these accounts to be factual. We can, however, find a great deal of moral insight and even personal inspiration when we read them for what they are: messages of spiritual instruction.

There are good reasons to conclude that the Jesus of history was interested in speaking either primarily or even exclusively to his own Galilean Jewish constituents. This is hinted at by the fact that the gospels talk about him visiting Judean communities and rarely mention Jesus in the larger Roman dominated cities. We, however, are only interested in how the Jesus tradition applies to modern society. A credible case can be made that the Jesus of history may have even been something of a racist on the basis of the exchange he had with the Syrophoenician woman whom he called a "dog" (Mark 7:25–30; Matt 15:21–28), but the Jesus tradition we choose to extoll teaches universal harmony. The historical Jesus may or may not have believed in an imminent apocalyptic end of history. If he did, he was wrong. Either way, we don't believe in an apocalypse by divine initiation, but we are still faced with potential forms of apocalypse from warfare, disease, pollution, or economic collapse. Any spiritual insight we can gain to help us avoid the real apocalyptic threats rather than the imaginary apocalypse of religious superstition is going to be of tremendous value to us.

The Jesus of the later church, once thoroughly turned into the spiritual Christ of "salvation from hell" myths, has been useful to both institutional religion and to empire-building governments. For progressives, such sordid mythology is the mental and emotional prison from which we have declared ourselves to have been liberated.

There are three things that I believe keep us tethered to Jesus. In order of ascending importance, I suggest that we continue to talk about Jesus because, first, the Christian traditions help us to understand ourselves through rituals around birth, coming of age, marriage, illness, and death, and in the processes of living within families and societies. Secondly, as I will discuss further in a later chapter, religion gives us a language set of stories and ideas that allows us to communicate with one another about meaningful living. For many of us, the Christian scriptures and traditions form an irreplaceable base of mutual understanding.

Finally, and most importantly, between the stripped-down view of the historical Jesus and the exalted presentation of the magical Christ stands a Jesus who is a loving advocate of the poor, sick, and vulnerable, and who challenges the power and abusive practices of the rich and of all empires.

The canonical gospels were written when the Roman Empire had already won its battle for dominance of the Judean region and, so far as they were concerned, of the known universe. Still we find—in subtle ways—a distinct anti-empire thread in how the gospels tell the story.

The exaggerated titles heaped upon Jesus in the evolving Christologies of Mark to Matthew and Luke and finally John can be seen as a distinct alternative to the empire and their enforced emperor worship. The titles of Savior, Son of God, and Lord were all given to the Roman Caesar. Even the tradition of virgin birth was given not only to powerful emperors but also to influential philosophers.

There is a distinct and undeniable way in which the Jesus tradition was offered as an alternative to cowering before wealth and power in the Roman Empire. There was a time for early Christians when saying that "Jesus is Lord" was a way of saying that "Caesar is not Lord." For many in the progressive movement, our identification with the teachings of Jesus is still a way of claiming an alternative way of living in the face of a modern empire that is comprised of both government and corporate power.

In our day, the coercion, deception, manipulation, and abuse of governments and corporations demands an alternative. A renewed devotion to the truth is the best antidote to the misdirection of corporate media. A spiritual sense of connection to the poor, war refugees, the uninsured, the uneducated, and the hopeless is the best response we can give to economic systems that continue to transfer resources that should be fairly spread among the people of the world into the hands of a smaller and smaller super-elite.

Jesus, as a teacher of radical compassion and self-sacrificing devotion to the truth, continues to be a symbol of the kind of spiritual depth we must claim as our own in order to transform the world in ways that bring good news to the poor and provide a bulwark against the abuses of the powerful.

5

What Are the Religions of the World to Us?

Mother, Mother, Mother! Everyone foolishly assumes that his clock
alone tells correct time. Christians claim to possess exclusive truth . . .
countless varieties of Hindus insist that their sect, no matter how small
and insignificant, expresses the ultimate position. Devout Muslims
maintain that Koranic revelation supersedes all others. The entire world
is being driven insane by this single phrase: "My religion alone is true."
O Mother, you have shown me that no clock is entirely accurate. Only
the transcendent sun of knowledge remains on time. Who can make
a system from Divine Mystery? But if any sincere practitioner, within
whatever culture or religion, prays, meditates with great devotion and
commitment to Truth alone, Your Grace will flood his mind and heart,
O Mother. His particular sacred tradition will be opened and illuminat-
ed. He will reach the one goal of spiritual evolution. Mother, Mother,
Mother! How I long to pray with sincere Christians in their churches
and to bow and prostrate with devoted Muslims in their mosques! All
religions are glorious![1]

—RAMAKRISHNA, A NINETEENTH-CENTURY
INDIAN HINDU MYSTIC

GARRISON KEILLOR ONCE HAD a regular skit on his radio show
A Prairie Home Companion about a guy named Bob who was
starting his own religion. He called it "Bobism," explaining that he

---

1. Quoted in Hixon, *Great Swan*, 15.

would have named it after his wife, Judy, but the name "Judaism" was already taken.

Of course, religions don't really start that way. Jesus didn't mean to start a new religion. He was, at most, a reformer of Judean religion. Even Islam, which claims to have a very specific beginning with a single founder, was, in any honest assessment, a reform movement that blended existing traditions.

The major world religions could all be compared to a mighty river that might be able to be traced to a specific original source, but by the time one becomes a real religion it will have drawn from hundreds and thousands of contributing sources. Given that four centuries passed between the life of Buddha and the written traditions of his teachings, it is safe to say that the Buddha would not recognize modern Buddhism. Similarly, Jesus would not likely recognize much of modern Christianity, nor would Moses recognize current Judaism. Muhammad would recognize a lot of the language of Islam, but you can bet that he would disown many modern practitioners.

Several influences factor into the birth of a religion. Every culture's religion became the repository of the wisdom and rules that seemed necessary for them to survive. Some parts of the kosher dietary laws of ancient Judaism had to do with their beliefs about what was healthy to eat and what was not good for you. These traditions also became ways that they distinguished themselves from surrounding rival tribes.

The Jews preserved their identity through generations specifically by keeping certain culturally unique rules about what you could wear, how you cut your hair, circumcision, and by what you could and could not eat. Their ritual religious practices and sacred texts identified them as being separate and apart from the Hittites, Philistines, and Canaanites. And you have to take your hat off to them because it isn't hard to find a Jewish community almost anywhere in the world, while you just don't hear much from the Hittites and Philistines anymore.

Religions evolve to meet the needs of a changing culture. As nomadic tribes became settled agrarian cultures, their rituals and lifestyle rules changed as well. Marital fidelity was important, not because the Creator of the universe has a vested interest in who is sleeping with whom but because the tribes needed to know who owned which farm and which vineyard. Property in Hebrew society followed patriarchal lines of inheritance so they needed to know who the father of any woman's child really was so that land ownership would not be contested. Therefore, a man could have lots of wives but a woman could only have one husband.

This is a least a part of the reason why we see such a double standard in the Hebrew Bible about marital infidelity for women and men. Male infidelity was sometimes treated fairly casually unless the sexual intercourse was with another man's wife. Proverbs 6:26 even makes male dalliance sound pretty cheap: "for a prostitute's fee is only a loaf of bread, but the wife of another stalks a man's very life." But as we see in Leviticus 20:10, "If a man commits adultery with the wife of his neighbor, both the adulterer and the adulteress shall be put to death." A great deal of our religious guilt, obsession with virginity, etc. has more to do with ancient real estate ownership than with Divine snooping into human bedrooms.

As the Semitic tribes became more settled and the land was divided among family owners, and having huge families became economically unwise, the practice of polygamy also went away. Ancient restrictions against homosexuality reinforced the need to have more babies so that you would always have an army to defend the nation against competing nations, and bearing children was celebrated as a sign of divine blessing. When it became economically disadvantageous to have huge families, such views began to evolve. Religious fundamentalism, devoted to religious values and practices that have long outlived their usefulness, became a liability to the world rather than a benefit.

Certainly, religious traditions about marriage and family also evolved to serve social needs. In the gospels, Jesus is reported to have condemned divorce, which would have protected women from what were then very abusive divorce practices. Women could be cast off in favor of a new wife, and they would likely get no property, support, or even access to their children. The early church, by condemning divorce, threw a cloak of protection around women in the first century, but in our time that condemnation of divorce has more often been used to force women to stay in abusive relationships under the entirely neurotic belief that God would condemn them to hell if they became unwilling to suffer any more beatings.

There is a line in the old hymn "Once to Every Man and Nation" that says, "time makes ancient good uncouth."[2] Practices institutionalized in religions to support community needs in one century can become lethal in another century. All religions evolve to adapt to their historical setting. This change is not a bad thing. In fact, it is a necessary thing. Therefore, we should not regard any of the world's religions as a rigidly static entity. Islam differs from Iran to Turkey just as it differs from the sixth century to the twenty-first century. The same can be said for Christianity, Judaism, Hinduism, and Buddhism.

Looking through the lens of academic historical criticism, we acknowledge that there were many authors in different centuries and different countries who had a hand in writing the first five books of the Hebrew Bible, even though most of us were emphatically told that they were written by one person, Moses. There may have been a historical prophetic liberator in Israel's ancient past named Moses, but Israelite religious texts were an evolving collection of wisdom and tradition that served an ancient tribal religious sect. Those writings were edited in dramatic ways both during their period of oral tradition and when they began to be recorded in written form.

Though most of us were taught as children to accept the Bible as a divine creation that has always been in its current form, this is clearly not true. Honest scholarship requires that we look at Scripture without preformed prejudices about either its accuracy or its origins. This awareness should help us to set aside our feelings of either religious superiority or of exclusivity when we consider the other religions of the world.

The same must be said about the Christian gospels. Our accounts of the teachings of Jesus are not stenographer's notes written

2. Lowell, "Once to Every Man."

down as Jesus spoke. The conclusion of the exhaustive work of the Jesus Seminar is that "Eighty-two percent of the words ascribed to Jesus in the gospels were not actually spoken by him."[3] The historical Jesus became the bulletin board onto which the early church posted their closely held beliefs and values. Christianity as it was practiced in the early church communities that gave us the gospel according to John would not have been just like the church that gave us Mark's gospel. The church in Jerusalem was not the same as the church in Antioch. Jesus did not invent Christianity, and the followers of Jesus did not pass along just one way of being Christian. There are many voices and perspectives in both the Old and the New Testament, and we should never assume that there is one orthodox perspective that trumps all of the others.

Every major religion of the world becomes a kind of language in which we tell our sacred stories, express our values, and pass along our morals. You would not say that French is right and German is wrong. There are things to like and things not to like about any language, but while one may be better than another for certain purposes, you cannot say that one entire language is just inherently better than another language, any more than you would say that one kind of music or one song is right and all others are wrong. You have your favorite songs, and there are probably kinds of music that you can't stand, but it doesn't take anything away from you when a member of your family has a different favorite song or if you can't stand the style of music that your children like the best. Islam does not have to be wrong so that Christianity can be right, and Hinduism as practiced in Bombay does not have to be like Hinduism as practiced in Portland, Oregon, for both to be Hinduism.

As I have previously pointed out, one of the real weaknesses of monotheism is its inherent investment in the belief that any one religion is so right that all other religions must be wrong. One of the things we really need to learn from Eastern religious traditions is the willingness to learn from all wisdom sources without having to be exclusively loyal to any one of them.

3. Funk, *Five Gospels*, 5.

Progressive Faith and Practice

My progressive faith was born in rural American Christianity, but my faith has been enhanced by my formal study of Islam and Judaism, of Buddhism and Hinduism. Though it is not difficult to point out places where the Mormon religious texts are absolutely hilariously absurd, there is also reason to envy the commonly very loving integrity of Mormon families. One could argue that Christian fundamentalists are often an oppressive danger to society, but we should also consider that their strict piety has been salvific for some people who could not otherwise control their appetites for drugs, alcohol, violence, crime, or sex.

A persuasive case can be made to argue that the exclusivism of Zoroastrianism, Judaism, Christianity, and Islam has been and still is a corrupting division in the world. It seems likely that all forms of sectarianism are counter to healthy spirituality, but that does not mean that it is helpful to condemn these religious traditions that are still mired in sectarian squabbles. As Madeline Albright argued in her book *The Mighty and the Almighty*, we need to work to encourage the better, the healthier, and the more helpful aspects within each religion.

It is demonstrably true that nearly all international terrorists, in this current time in history, claim an aspect of Muslim faith. But Islam is not an inherently violent religion. In fact, it can be a source of inspiration for both international peace and individual charity towards the poor. Christianity doesn't always have to be misogynistic, homophobic, militaristic, or even in bed with out-of-control capitalism and the political right. Christianity can be a source of compassion, mercy, forgiveness, peace, and passion for justice.

Religious tolerance should not be mistaken for tolerance of abusive, oppressive, and neurotic religions. We do well to confront, reject, correct, and refuse to tolerate any aspect of a religion that perpetuates gender or racial prejudice, or that seeks to convert, control, or dominate those who do not adhere to its sectarian views. For example, we should not just passively accept Catholic and Baptist discrimination against women, gays, and lesbians. No one should use religion as a means of legitimizing his or her abusive prejudices any more than being a member of the KKK would make it acceptable to be a racist.

Most religions have their origin in countercultural movements intended to defend and improve the lives of the very poor and oppressed. You can certainly see how Muhammad was attempting to rescue his people from chaotic and violent circumstances. Jesus specifically sought out the poor and outcast of a people whose land was occupied by a militaristic empire. In as much as the Moses story is rooted in some history, he was portrayed as a liberator of slaves, who led them from bondage to independence.

Yet each of these great world religions was eventually co-opted by governments and institutions of religion that used people's faith to control them. Still, there remains in each faith the roots of slave rebellion, a yearning for liberty, self-determination, and meaningful living. That is our real spiritual inheritance, and that is what progressive faith must restore to adherents of all world religions. There is no reason not to learn from one another just as there is no defense for trying to convert one another.

No Muslim needs to become Christian; they just need to be a good Muslim. And no Christian needs to become a Jew; they just need to be a healthy and open-minded Christian. Every religion has things both in creed and history for which repentance is the only appropriate response, but each also contains the seeds of hope for a better future. We progressives are not rejecting our religious heritage; we're just deciding that we are going to get healthy.

6

What Is Church, Synagogue, Mosque, or Temple to Us Now?

We are all connected to each other biologically, to the earth chemically, to the rest of the universe atomically.[1]

—NEIL DEGRASSE TYSON

M. SCOTT PECK, THE late psychiatrist and self-help author, wrote a book about creating community entitled *A Different Drum*. It is regrettably dated, having been written in the midst of the Cold War. However, his chapter on "Patterns of Transformation"[2] is as helpful as anything in his more famous book, *The Road Less Traveled*. He describes the movement from childhood chaos into institutional, dogmatic religion followed by a time of questioning and doubt. The persistent and the fortunate find their way beyond that emptiness into a fourth stage of spiritual evolution, one that is a more mystical approach to faith that offers a synthesis between what can be known and the sense of awe and wonder associated with a spiritual perspective on life.

Please allow me to give you a too brief summation of Peck's observations: Children are born into a frightening universe full of giants and in which they have little or no control over anything

1. Tyson, "We Are All Connected."
2. Peck, *Different Drum*, 186–208.

that happens to them. In many instances, they resolve the fears of early childhood through incorporation into a formal, institutional religion that gives them solid answers to the big questions of life and very distinct marching orders about how to live in a way that makes you one of God's best friends and avoids any eternal conflict with the universe.

Those answers, however, don't hold much water when they are critically examined. Most people do not dismiss them outright, but they move their importance way down so that they can remain tacitly Jewish, Christian, or Muslim, and in that way they hold on to a bit of divine fire insurance without letting institutional religion mess their lives up too much. If people took traditional Christianity literally, we would see a lot of people selling everything they own, giving the proceeds to the poor, and living their lives like ascetic monks. But we, in fact, rarely see anything other than symbolic devotion to the weightier demands of traditional faith. Most people hold on to a symbolic fragment of religion, sometimes using it to excuse their own failings and sometimes using it to pass judgment on others—but rarely allowing it to change their own lives to any significant degree.

Sadly, most institutions of religion are fairly happy with this arrangement. They are holding on to members who at least visit occasionally and offer some financial support and good will that allows for the institution's continued existence. But the more persistent critical thinkers will find the courage to swim against the current of family and society and be entirely dismissive of the truth claims associated with religion.

Most of Western Europe and coastal North America have arrived at this third stage. Middle America is gradually following suit. That was certainly Scott Peck's own journey through his childhood and evolving awareness in medical school and psychiatric training. But he was one of the ones who were not willing simply to live in perpetual skeptical individualism. He pressed on to find a faith that embraced both science and a more mystical awareness of our connectedness to one another and to the universe.

I had the chance to have a brief personal conversation with Peck in the late 1980s. He advised me to get out of the ministry as soon as I could. He said, "There is no spirit left in the institutional church. You need to find a better way to help build community in the world than you can possibly do in a church." It was not the advice I was expecting from him and now, more than twenty-five years later, I think that I can say that he was both right and wrong.

I don't have much hope for denominational Christianity or in much of what goes on in the institutional mosques, synagogues, and churches of the twenty-first century unless they are willing to undergo radical transformation. They cannot have a future while they remain attached to ancient myths that fly in the face of modern science.

Institutions of religion tend to discourage critical thinking in favor of unquestioning loyalty. Even many churches that publicly advertise that they are open to those who doubt or question seem to have a fairly short period of tolerance before some level of conformity to traditional superstition and magic is expected of them.

It is horribly disappointing that so many great minds were presented, early in their lives, with a choice between reason and belief, between religious superstition and science. Richard Dawkins said that he was raised in the Anglican Church and left when he was in his mid-teens. He realized that the theory of evolution presented a more plausible explanation than traditional religion for how the world came to be in its current. He not only abandoned faith in favor of science, but he has also devoted passionate energy to publishing aggressive attacks on religion, imploring other people to give up on faith entirely.

He said, "There is a new wave of reason sweeping across America, Britain, Europe, Australia, South America, the Middle East and Africa where superstition had a firm hold."[3] I hope that he is right, but I do not believe that a wave of reason needs to sweep away all forms of spiritual community. In fact, I am depending on that wave of reason to help us to become healthy again.

3. Dawkins, *Symphony of Science.*

But Dawkins is not alone in turning his back on religion in favor of rational thought and scientific inquiry. Recognizing that the religion of our parents and the doctrinal claims of traditional Judaism, Christianity, and Islam simply do not stand up to the light of reason necessarily gives us an experience of loss. It is not that traditional religion has no value. In truth, it had tremendous value to us at one point in our lives, and we give it up with a lot of weeping and gnashing of teeth!

Most days I talk or correspond with people who are both hurt and angry that they have been lied to, deceived, manipulated, and made to feel guilt, shame, and fear by religious authorities, family members, and friends. And yet, they still somehow want to salvage something of their faith tradition. One can hardly blame the victims of formal religion for having trust issues. The question becomes, can we offer a viable spiritual alternative before they give up on faith entirely?

It is understandable that when you realize what a mental prison religious superstition has been that you want to run away and have nothing to do with anything that uses the language of church, synagogue, mosque, or temple ever again. At the risk of sounding a bit ironic, I believe that the future of the church is absolutely dependent upon large numbers of people adamantly rejecting and vacating the institutions that have perpetuated these Iron Age myths.

It is difficult for anyone to receive what progressive faith has to offer until they have the courage to let go of the security blanket of a familiar though outgrown religion. Most of the members of the progressive congregation where I am the pastor spent several years in that "in between" region, having left traditional churches and having little reason to go in search of a corporate religious life that was simultaneously rational and yet open to spiritual perspectives. Only gradually have my peers allowed themselves to reconsider being part of an organization that might be defined as a church.For many of us the question of "Why bother with any kind of church or spiritual community?" is one with no clear answer. When I left denominational ministry, I vowed never to set foot in a church again, and I am not entirely free of those sentiments even as I write this book. Institutions of religion have promoted wars and violent oppression of the poor, minorities, women, homosexuals, the divorced, and even those who were just free thinkers. The victims of religion number in the billions, even today, as gay people try to live straight lives to conform to the expectations of their faith communities, driving many to suicide, substance abuse, infidelity, and violence. Women stay in abusive marriages because their church claims not to "believe in divorce," which must rank as one of the most absurd forms of bondage imposed on the victims of organized religion. A farmer in Oklahoma may not "believe in tornados" but that refusal to believe will not prevent his barn from being blown into the next county.

Young men and women have their critical thinking skills curtailed by religious insistence upon forcing themselves to pretend to believe what is clearly not rational. The young grow up with confused feelings of self-loathing, fear of their own bodies, and neurotic guilt for having feelings and appetites that are purely human. And that is before we even get into the matters of church politics, where so many of us have been emotionally and economically tortured as employees of the church.

What brought me back to church was a need to be connected. Humans are pack animals, after all. We have an existential longing to be connected to one another, even though, after millions of years of evolution, we do not appear to be especially good at doing it.

The last few years that I was in the employ of a traditional church, I found most of the meaning of my career in the relief work we were doing on the Louisiana coast with Hurricane Katrina victims and among the poor of rural Nicaragua. When I left parish ministry, I found that I listened to the news with an entirely different perspective. In the days following Katrina's devastating landfall on the gulf coast, I was able to pull together a team of volunteers, raise financial support, and head down to the coast to help. As an individual, learning of natural disasters produced sorrow and sympathy but left me without any reasonable means of personally responding beyond my meager individual ability to send contributions.

No one was more surprised to see me back in parish ministry than I was, but it was the deep need to be in community that made me willing to try again. In community, I am able to be involved in a collective effort at delivering direct aid to victims and in corporate opposition to the institutions that sponsor injustice. At this time, I am a part of a volunteer team that takes hot meals to hundreds of the unsheltered homeless of my hometown every week. On my own, my efforts would be, at best, symbolic and sporadic. In community, we encourage one another, inspire one another, and plan together so that any Thursday or Friday morning of the week our church is found among the most desperately poor of our city.

The comedian Jon Stewart has said, "If you don't stick to your values when they're being tested, they're not values: they're hobbies."[4] I am afraid that in most cases, when we are not a part of community, our convictions largely reside in our own heads. They are not even hobbies; they are just opinions.

They may be passionately held and expressed opinions, but they are much less likely to become meaningful action unless we are united with others of similar convictions. I am confident that if the congregation I now serve as pastor suddenly ceased to exist that most of the good work we do for the poor of our city would just stop happening. We remain disciplined in meaningful service only because we remain in contact with one another. Those who abandon the church may have views and opinions very similar to ours, but as loners those rugged individualists are of little use in actually doing anything. There are, of course, wonderful exceptions to this seen in individuals who live lives of service and sacrifice to others without being in community. I'm just convinced that I don't have what it would take to keep up an active life of involvement without my community connections.

There is a further benefit of being in community—and I must ask for some grace in how I am going to say this: There are very

4. Stewart, "Jon Stewart Quotes."

few things that I can claim as being original to me but I have a theory of psychology that is my own. And to get the full impact of it, I need to ask for your permission to say it in a rather crass way. I call it my "asshole theory." It is this: Everyone will be just as much of a jerk as the people around him or her will allow. Without close community with others, we can all become pretty self-centered and self-serving jerks.

In the academic world, we champion the concept of "peer review." That is, anything you discover in research or come up with in terms of your own theorizing or creation must be subjected to the critical review of other professionals in your field. Peer review is not perfect because sometimes your peers are jerks themselves. But any substantive progress in science, medicine, physics, and, I would also argue, even in art and literature is dependent upon peer review. We need each other to "provoke one another to love and good deeds" (Heb 10:24b), to check one another when our egos or our ideas become irrational or narcissistic.

Being in a faith community keeps us in a kind of peer review. Buddhism teaches that the greatest of illusions is our sense of separation. Interesting then that scientists—specifically, physicists—are starting to sound like Buddha when they speak of how connected we all are. I believe that the church has a future because it can be an expression of that great human connection and because when we are connected we really can change the world for the better, and in the process we will inevitably find that we are also personally being changed for the better.

And that, my friends, is not something that will happen on Twitter or Facebook. I'm staying in church because I need it and, as irritating as I can be, I sense that at times others need me too. Together we will become better people while we help to give birth to a better world.

7

What Do We Do When We Gather as a Community?

This has to be said; so let it now be said. Whoever you are, whatever in other respects your life may be, my friend, by ceasing to take part in the public worship of God, as it now is, you have constantly one guilt the less, and that a great one: you do not take part in treating God as a fool . . .[1]

—SØREN KIERKEGAARD

Christian liturgy should intensify the "cognitive dissonance" between the community of faith and the world surrounding it.[2]

—RICHARD JOHN NEUHAUS

THE PROGRESSIVE CHURCH THAT has been the laboratory for the writing of this book began with a couple of dozen people meeting on Sunday evenings to talk about why they didn't go to church anymore and to consider what they could do with their spiritual instincts. They read books together about religion and social justice. They were political and social liberals, they were religious progressives, and so they had little difficulty in setting aside tra-

1. Kierkegaard, "This Must Be Said."
2. Neuhaus, *Catholic Moment*, 65.

ditional Christian beliefs and embracing a critical approach to the Bible and the historical Jesus.

Our small group quickly and easily agreed on the priorities that should be a part of any spiritual community: working to save the planet; fighting poverty and prejudice; working for the civil rights of minorities, gays, and lesbians, and immigrants; and working for international peace and interfaith dialogue. With each essential priority we named, there was always at least a little bit of looking backwards. We talked about how the churches we had left had disappointed us in these areas, and we tried to name what was valuable about our journey that we wanted desperately to retain.

After several weeks of conversations, one brave lady stood up and asked in a very demanding way, "Why don't we just start our own church?" A bit of electricity moved through the room, but it died out just as quickly when I began to ask my friends what we would do when our new church gathered.

Would we sing hymns? If so, what kind of songs would we sing? Would we have corporate prayers? Would we practice communion, baptism, or any other sacramental or ritual observances? In a group of about twenty people, it became evident that we couldn't get more than three or four to attend any church service that we could design.

Trying to design an order of service may seem to be much less interesting that fighting social injustice or debating our beliefs about the character of the historical Jesus, but if your intention is to create communities around progressive faith, this will be the highest hurdle you have to jump. After several months of conversation, we decided that we would give starting a church a try. Looking back over these past six years, we have rarely disagreed on matters of mission, purpose, outreach, or demonstration but we have squabbled about the content of the liturgy.

Our experience parallels much of what has been documented in other new church starts. There was a lot of coming and going in the first two years for all of the reasons we had identified in our prechurch conversations. There were those who wanted a church that was open and affirming, pro-marriage rights, etc. but who still wanted pretty traditional evangelical theology and practice. Others were quite firm in their post-theistic views and were quickly disdainful of any religious ritual or use of words such as "worship" or "Lord" that had followed us from our traditional roots.

I have no uniform service suggestion to make here for how progressive churches should gather. When we started our small congregation, our first service looked a lot like my last service in a formal denominational worship service. My theology had evolved, but my habits took longer to change and they are, in fact, still changing.

Though we had some interfaith and no-faith participants from the start, most of the members of this initial group came from Catholic or Protestant traditions. Both consciously and unconsciously, we brought some assumptions with us about what it meant to have a church service. My liturgy professor at Vanderbilt was a strict, formal, high church Presbyterian who could be aptly described with the words John Steinbeck used to describe Liza Hamilton in *East of Eden*: ". . . a tight hard little woman humorless as a chicken. She had a dour Presbyterian mind and code of morals that pinned down and beat the brains out of nearly everything that was pleasant to do."[3]

For twenty-five years I was a liturgical purist, adhering to the formal traditions of the church and rejecting all forms of syncretism with American culture. I have no excuse for why it took me so long to realize how absurd this was. The ancient church seasons and holidays were predicated on the harvests and traditional observances of the cultures that gave birth to them. The timing of the spring wheat harvest in Palestine, which is the root of the early celebration of Pentecost, should not carry more weight with us than our nation's observance of Memorial Day, Labor Day, Thanksgiving, or even Mothers' Day.

A fellow student once tried to insist on the observance of Mother's Day in church and our professor shot back, "Did your mother die on the cross for you?" That was a real showstopper in

---

3. Steinbeck, *East of Eden*, 8.

the classroom. If I could relive that moment, I would have said, "No, but then Jesus didn't either." There is good reason to not let greeting card holidays control the content of our gatherings but there is also good reason not to cave in to ancient views of theology that we have summarily rejected. As we seek to have substantive and relevant services, if the entire nation's mind is geared towards a national holiday or a recent event of great importance, it would be ignoring the opportunity of a teachable moment to pass by that topic. Thanksgiving and Mothers' Day do not have to be either nationalistic or solipsistic. Does a pastor have anything of importance to say regarding modern families, which are currently under many kinds of social pressure? If he or she does, then by all means, speak up! Does the preacher have a prophetic word to say about national life on Thanksgiving or Independence Day? Then for goodness' sake, stand up and say it! While the church should be in tension with culture, it does not exist outside of culture. In fact, the tunes of many popular hymns were not sacred in origin; some were even quite colorful drinking songs in their earliest incarnations. We owe no fealty to hymns that, though familiar to us, articulate a theology contrary to our own. The issue is to find some balance in which we give ourselves permission to honor our heritage while being free to grow, learn, and change.

One of the great architects of progressive thinking is Bishop John Shelby Spong, who still often appears in public in the clerical collar he wore as an Episcopal bishop. Marcus Borg, who has done as much as any author alive today to demythologize our understanding of the historical Jesus, still speaks in very devotional Christian language. It is entirely possible to live within the language and ritual universe of the traditional church while infusing it with new and more realistic interpretations.

In the church where I am the pastor, we have slowly evolved away from much of the language and formal practice of the church traditions of our past. We never sang the traditional doxology, but we did sing a gender-inclusive version of it until a member of the church asked, "Why are we singing a Trinitarian song if we don't believe in Trinitarian theology?" There was no rational explanation beyond the fact that none of us had ever consciously thought about the Trinitarian nature of the doxology.

We have since written new lyrics to replace the Trinitarian language of the old doxology that are focused on our faith community, but the new version doesn't pack the nostalgic punch of the more traditional one and, as some have observed, without some vestiges of our former experience our gatherings do not "feel like church." Still, the next generation of progressives will not likely want to hold on to theologically sanitized hymns and prayers. My suspicion is that they will not continue our observances of Communion, they will probably not want a hymnal at all, nor will they preserve the cross or the clerical vestments that some of us still need to make our gatherings look and feel enough like what we associate with the practice of faith to stay connected to our community.

We freely blend the reading of Scripture with the public reading of passages of philosophy, theology, science, or other wisdom sources. We blend traditional religious music with secular music. And though we primarily come from Christian roots we now also blend the literature and conventions of all world religions in our gatherings because we are trying to foster and strengthen our spirituality but not our sectarianism.

We may be one of the only progressive churches in the world that begins our Sunday service with a chanted Psalm text. I have argued in favor of holding on to this because, for me, it marks the movement from ordinary time into a time when the community is gathered for the specific purpose of being the church. We still have congregational singing and prayers because, for us, the blending of our voices in unison is a way of both becoming and expressing community.

Our service maintains the traditional fourfold movement of formal liturgy: gathering, proclamation, thanksgiving, and going to serve; though any one of its parts would seem rather different from what anyone would experience in a Catholic, Episcopal, or Lutheran church. We avoid the use of such words as "praise" and "worship" because we do not believe that there is an ego-deficient

Deity enthroned in the clouds who needs, wants, or would enjoy our worship and praise. We strive to avoid religious language that would in any way encourage or institutionalize gender or sexual prejudice, dominance, or triumphalism—which, of course, cuts out most of the hymns we know by heart!

This is the basic outline of a Sunday morning service:

The Gathering of God's People

Prelude

Psalm Chant

*Gathering Hymn

*Prayer of Confession

*Assurance of Hope

*Passing of the Peace

*Shared Blessing:

> "Blessed be God's faith community
> By grace called forth in unity
> T'ward truth and justice daily move
> Through service brave inspired by love. Amen."

Proclamation

Wisdom Lesson

Sermon

Anthem

Thanksgiving

Offertory Sentence

Offertory

Invitation to Communion

Communion Hymn

Community Prayer

Sharing of the Elements

Charge to be a Blessing to the World

*Benediction:

Pastor: Go in peace to love and serve!

People: Thanks be to God!

*Hymn of Departure

Postlude

What would have been called "secular" music in my formal liturgy classes years ago seems now more likely to convey the social justice message that is at the center of our prophetic witness. Protest songs, union organizing songs, civil rights lyrics, and anti-war songs seem to give voice to the message we are trying to represent to the world much better than most of our traditional hymns. Pete Seeger wrote and performed music intended to call disciples into the movement for peace, social justice, and racial harmony from the early part of the last century and into the first years of this century. His banjo bore an inscription that read, "This machine surrounds hatred and forces it to surrender."[4]

That's the kind of music that should be sung in progressive churches. This is a partial list of what we have used in recent months:

Music List by Artist:

Beatles "All You Need Is Love"

Bev Grant "We Were There"

Billie Holliday "God Bless the Child"

Billy Bragg "Do unto Others"

4. Rosen, "This Machine Surrounds."

Billy Bragg "Tomorrow's Gonna be a Better Day"

Black Eyed Peas "Where Is the Love?"

Bob Dylan "Blind Willie McTell"

Bob Dylan "Chimes of Freedom"

Bob Dylan "Times They Are a-Changin'"

Bob Dylan "When the Ship Comes in"

Bob Marley "Get Up, Stand Up"

Bob Marley "One Love"

Bob Marley "Redemption Song"

Bob Marley "Stiff Necked Fools"

Bob Marley "Wisdom"

Billy Joel "2000 Years"

Billy Joel "We Didn't Start the Fire"

Brett Dennen "Ain't No Reason"

Bruce Cockburn "Iesus Ahatonnia"

Bruce Cockburn "Lovers in a Dangerous Time"

Bruce Cockburn "Nicaragua"

Burt Bacharach ""What the World Needs Now"

Chi-Lites "(For God's Sake) Give More Power to the People"

Cat Stevens "Peace Train"

Curtis Mayfield and The Impressions "People Get Ready"

Dallas Jones "Finally Crossed the Line"

Dallas Jones "Wherever You Roam"

David Greathouse "The Sound That Love Makes"

David Mallett "The Garden Song (Inch by Inch)"

David Wilcox "Fearless Love"

David Wilcox "Jesus Ruins Christmas"

David Wilcox "Show the Way"

David Wilcox "To Love"

Dennis Lambert/Brian Potter "One Tin Soldier"

Dion "Abraham, Martin, and John"

Don Henley "Dirty Laundry"

Eric Bogle "No Man's Land"

Everlast "What It's Like"

Floyd Collins (musical) "How Glory Goes"

George Gershwin "It Ain't Necessarily So"

George Harrison "Give Me Love"

Gil Turner "Carry It On"

Graham Nash "In Your Name"

Greg Greenway "Standing on the Side of Love"

Hair (musical) "Easy to Be Hard"

Hairspray (musical) "Where I've Been"

Harold Melvin and The Blue Notes "Wake Up, Everybody"

Holly Near "I Ain't Afraid"

Hunchback of Notre Dame (musical) "God Help the Outcasts"

Indigo Girls "Philosophy of Loss"

Into the Woods (musical) "Children Will Listen"

Into the Woods (musical) "No One Is Alone"

Iris Dement "He Reached Down"

Iris Dement "Let the Mystery Be"

Iris Dement "Wasteland of the Free"

Jack Johnson "Gone"

Jackson Browne "Alive in the World"

Jackson Browne "Don't You Want to Be There"

Jackson Browne "Far from the Arms of Hunger"

Jackson Browne "It Is One"

Jackson Browne "Rebel Jesus"

Jacques Brel "If We Only Have Love"

Jakob Dylan "Evil Is Alive and Well"

James Taylor "Shower the People You Love with Love"

Jason Robert Brown "Christmas Lullaby"

Jesus Christ Superstar (musical) "Heaven on Their Minds"

Joe Hill "The Preacher and the Slave"

John Bell "Inspired by Love and Anger"

John Mayer "Love Is a Verb"

John Mayer "Waiting on the World to Change"

John Lennon "Give Peace a Chance"

John Lennon "Happy Xmas/War Is Over"

John Lennon "Imagine"

John Prine "Paradise"

John Prine "Your Flag Decal Won't Get You into Heaven Anymore"

Johnny Cash "What on Earth (Will You Do for Heaven's Sake)"

Johnny Lang "Leaving to Stay"

Joni Mitchell "Big Yellow Taxi"

Julie Gold "From a Distance"

Kelley Hunt "The Next Step"

Kool Moe Dee "Funke Wisdom"

Langhorn Slim "Be Set Free"

Leonard Bernstein "So Pretty"

Leonard Cohen "Everybody Knows"

Leonard Cohen "Hallelujah"

Lisa Loeb "Falling in Love"

Little Steven "I Am a Patriot"

Mahalia Jackson "If I Can Help Somebody"

Mahalia Jackson "It Don't Cost Very Much"

Malvina Reynolds "From Way Up Here"

Malvina Reynolds "God Bless the Grass"

Malvina Reynolds "It Isn't Nice"

Malvina Reynolds "Jesus Was a Saviour, Too"

Malvina Reynolds "Magic Penny (Love Is Something)"

Malvina Reynolds "Sing Along"

Malvina Reynolds "We Hate to See Them Go"

Martin Sexton "My Faith Is Gone"

Martin Sexton "The Shape of Things to Come"

Mary Chapin Carpenter "Come Darkness, Come Light"

Mason Proffit "Two Hangmen"

Melissa Etheridge "I Need to Wake Up"

Michael Franti "Hello, Bonjour"

Mike + The Mechanics "The Living Years"

Mimi Farina "Bread and Roses"

Neil Young "When God Made Me"

Nick Lowe "(What's So Funny 'Bout) Peace, Love, and Understanding"

Paul Kelly "Special Treatment"

Paul Simon "Blessed"

Paul Simon "Father and Daughter"

Patty Griffin "Up to the Mountain"

Pete Seeger "If I Had a Hammer"

Pete Seeger "Take it from Dr. King"

Peter Gabriel "Shaking the Tree"

Peter, Paul, and Mary "Rich Man, Poor Man"

Porter Wagoner/Jeff Buckley "A Satisfied Mind"

Ragtime (musical) "Make Them Hear You"

Randy Newman "Piece of the Pie"

R. C. Clarke "The Blind Ploughman"

Rebel Diaz "Which Side Are You On?"

Red Hot Chili Peppers "Shallow Be Thy Game"

Rob Thomas "Street Corner Symphony"

Roche Sisters "Anyway"

Roddy Barnes "A Better World"

Ron Sexsmith "Gold in Them Hills"

Sam Cooke "A Change Is Gonna Come"

Sarah Crews "What You Preach"

Sarah McLachlan "Prayer of St. Francis of Assisi"

Sly and the Family Stone "Everyday People"

Solomon Burke "None of Us Are Free"

South Pacific (musical) "You've Got to Be Carefully Taught"

Stephen Foster "Hard Times Come Again No More"

Stevie Wonder "Free"

Stevie Wonder "Heaven Help Us All"

Stevie Wonder "Heaven Is Ten Zillion Light Years Away"

Stevie Wonder "Higher Ground"

Stevie Wonder "Love's in Need of Love Today"

Stevie Wonder "Someday at Christmas"

Stevie Wonder "You Haven't Done Nothin'"
Sting "If I Ever Lose My Faith in You"
Styx "Show Me the Way"
Sy Miller/Jill Jackson "Let There Be Peace on Earth"
Todd Rundgren "Love Is the Answer"
Tom Morello "World Wide Rebel Songs"
Tom Waits "Come on Up to the House"
Tom Waits "Georgia Lee"
Tom Waits "The House Where Nobody Lives"
U2 "One"
U2 "Pride (In the Name of Love)"
Virgil Thomson "The Divine Image"
Weird Al "Eat It"
Woody Guthrie "Jesus Christ"
Ziggy Marley "Love Is My Religion"

While many progressive churches have given up on offering classes or even including sermons in their services, we have doubled down on both. We believe that the teaching function of the faith community is central. We cut a lot of corners to save money but we have invested heavily in guest lecturers and seminars because we are convinced that critical thinking and a well-informed membership are vital to our success.

As the progressive movement was starting to find its legs at the end of the twentieth century, two books made an important impression on me. The first was a little volume by Leander Keck entitled *The Church Confident*, and the second was Marva Dawn's *Reaching Out without Dumbing Down*. Both argued that our gatherings should be theologically rich, instructive, and intelligent and that we should strive for excellence. Keck very specifically decried the lack of beauty in the world and pleaded with us to infuse our gatherings with art, music, poetry, and even architecture that can feed our starving souls and, indeed, astonish us in a way that change us, that enlarge our vision and awareness.[5] Though they

5. Keck, *Church Confident*, 25.

did not quote the Great Dane, Søren Kierkegaard, I think that both Dawn and Keck would have said "Amen" to Kierkegaard when he praised those who had stopped going to church because, in refraining from attending public worship as it was in his day, they were at least avoiding publicly insulting God.

Our gatherings, by the simple fact that we are gathering, promote the building of community. Some of the most important parts of our Sunday mornings take place around the coffee pots and in the church aisles. If orthopraxy (right actions) is to be preferred over orthodoxy (right beliefs), then surely the first priority of a spiritual orthopraxy is that we love one another. It is difficult to imagine any kind of congregational success that would be laudable in absence of community affection. Our gatherings should nurture friendships and break down the walls of indifference and anonymity. The language we speak to one another should be obviously seasoned with sincere love and a cherishing of one another's humanity.

But what happens between prelude and postlude should include instruction, inspiration, and moral challenge. While much of what happens under steeples in America seems intent upon slowly killing parishioners with boredom, Richard John Neuhaus said, as mentioned above, that "liturgy should intensify the 'cognitive dissonance' between the community of faith and the world surrounding it."

There are things going on in the world about which we should be shocked, grief stricken, and provoked to action. Most of those things will never make it into the corporate media but shouldn't they make it into the liturgy?

On a perfect Sunday, those who attend a church service have a reasonable expectation that they will learn something, experience a sense of awe and wonder, and leave feeling more closely connected to one another and more determined to go into the coming week prepared to bear prophetic witness for justice and to serve in sacrificial and meaningful ways to bring healing to the world. Realistically, we will not get all three every week, but if we consistently fail to get one or two of them then shouldn't we turn our church buildings into something more useful, like a used car lot or a flea market?

The modern church should take its prophetic voice in society seriously. If churches lack the courage and insight to be prophetic, they should at least be of service in an exemplary manner. But the old saying that you should either "lead, follow, or get out of the way" applies nowhere more than it applies to churches.

8

Shall We Still Pray?

Prayer does not change God, but it changes him who prays.[1]

—SØREN KIERKEGAARD

"Substance over symbolism" is one of my regular mantras. I am convinced that religious symbolism is often used, not as a teaching tool, but to take the place of substance. What is, after all, lighting a candle in honor of abused children compared with volunteering to become a foster parent? Religious people have been trained through practice to make symbolic actions and to then tell themselves that they have done something. This idea is nowhere more true than when it comes to the way that we speak about prayer.

I said to my congregation, in a sermon about prayer, that telling someone that you would pray for them was the same thing as saying, "I have no intentions of actually doing anything to help you." What, after all, is praying for someone to get well compared with bringing them a steaming pot of chicken soup?

Just a couple of days after delivering that sermon, my father died in his home five hundred miles from my church home. My congregants couldn't attend the funeral, nor could they directly express their sympathy in the language of the church, which is usually a covered dish. I speak "covered dish" and gladly accept

---

1. Kierkegaard, "Prayer Does Not Change."

that homemade food is the physical equivalent of love. The normal church response would have been to have called or emailed to say, "You are in my prayers," or the modern, tacitly more secular version, "You are in my thoughts and prayers." I suppose adding "thoughts" is a way that we can hedge our bets against the supernatural theism implied in intercessory prayer but, because of what I had said, my friends were nervous even about that.

We no longer say intercessory prayers in our public services because we do not believe that God works like a giant Santa Claus in the clouds. But that is not to say that progressives have abandoned the practice of prayer. As Kierkegaard said so succinctly, prayer does not change the one to whom we pray but it does change the one who prays. We do not pray in order to give God information that God might not have known, nor do we assume that God is some kind of an ogre who must be pestered into charitable action.

In the literature of Alcoholics Anonymous, people who are in recovery are encouraged to increase their conscious contact with God as they understand God. Even the ancient mystics of Christian spirituality spoke with disdain about prayer that was either supplication or intercession or even prayer that used words. Let me briefly describe three types of prayer. First, there are discursive prayers, verbal prayers such as what we say in public or perhaps at our dinner tables. Then there is meditation and contemplation. There is no general agreement in the distinctions that I am making, but for my own purposes, when I say that I am meditating that means that I am thinking about something, while if I attempt contemplation I am specifically and intentionally silent, and I am striving not to think about anything at all.

Discursive prayer is basically where everyone starts, whether that is repeating a rote prayer, reading one written in a liturgy, or composing one's own feelings and thoughts in words. The act of praying is an acknowledgement of our spiritual worldview, of our connection to one another, to God, and to the universe. Discursive prayers can be prayers of praise, confession, or thanksgiving, but most commonly they are prayers of intercession.

Western Christians can learn something very important from the perspective of Buddhism with regard to the essence of prayer. The four noble truths of Buddhism teach:

First, life is full of suffering. Secondly, suffering comes from our desires, our attachments. Thirdly, the end of suffering comes from learning to let go of our attachments, to learn how not to desire or love things. The fourth noble truth is the invitation to follow the way of the Buddha in prayerful contemplation (called the Eightfold Path).

Though I intellectually discourage praying "for" something, I don't want to be dishonest. Like most people, whenever I am scared or worried I still find myself reflexively praying for divine intervention. Mahatma Gandhi said, "Prayer is not asking. It is a longing of the soul. It is daily admission of one's weakness. It is better in prayer to have a heart without words than words without a heart."[2] The fact is that we love some people so intensely that when they are in trouble our sincere hope will become desperate prayer on their behalf.

I don't believe that my silent prayers work in the way that we were taught to believe when we were children. Regardless of my intellectual beliefs, my anxieties about my loved ones or fears for myself manage to get composed into earnest prayer as naturally as the way our bodies will produce adrenaline when we see a barking dog charging at us. I think that is normal, but we should not let it recapture our minds and bring us once more into the prison of magical thinking. When we speak of prayer, I hope that we will concentrate on the kind of prayer that really can change the one who prays.

Meditation is a form of prayer similar to what Buddhists mean when they speak of "mindfulness." In fact, we have examples of parallels between Buddhist "mindful walking" and the Christian practice of praying the Stations of the Cross or meditatively walking a labyrinth. Trappist monks today typically have a small crucifix on the wall of their cell and a simple icon, either of which

2. Gandhi, "Prayer Is Not Asking."

can be the focus for hours of meditation. A person in meditation is striving to think deeply, prayerfully, about one thing.

Many people will take a single verse of Scripture and reflect on it during a long meditative walk. During my graduate school years, when Scripture was too closely associated with my academic work for me peacefully and calmly to meditate on a verse from the Bible, it was my habit to read through the sayings of the desert fathers (and mothers) until I could find a single sentence that was meaningful to me and then I would spend hours walking through the grounds of the monastery where I went on retreat just thinking about that sentence.

During most of our waking hours we are either thinking about the past or anticipating the future. Meditation is a way of becoming centered again in the present moment. In recent years I have discovered much of the calming and centering effect of my former monastic prayer retreats in my weekly practice of yoga.

I don't know if everyone else in my yoga class has to concentrate anything like as hard as I do to achieve some of those challenging positions, but I have found yoga to be an excellent means towards meditation and I do not hesitate to call it "prayer." Again, some people may simply be exercising just as someone might just be taking a walk, but either activity done intentionally, mindfully, as meditative prayer can make the experience something that strengthens our spiritual awareness.

Finally, there is what we call contemplation. Contemplative prayer might be the most unlikely and yet the most needed in our modern society. Many of us can scarcely so much as go to the bathroom without the company of our smart phones or tablets. My generation has gone from three channels on a black-and-white TV set in the living room to having media in endless varieties in every room and even in our pockets. Silence has become nearly intolerable. We have to have something to distract us, entertain us, and to make certain that we are never simply alone and still.

We have twenty-four-hour news channels, though none of them have more than thirty minutes of hard news in a day— it is mostly fluff, distraction. We hear more about Miley Cyrus' twerking butt than we know about why there is a civil war raging in Syria. We have the world's knowledge at our fingertips on the Internet but a large portion of traffic online is still just pornography. For the most part, our distractions fill our time, our minds, our souls, and our character with junk, maybe even poison.

There is an old story, handed down in many different forms, about a young novitiate pestering the abbot of his monastery asking, "Father, how can I draw near to God?" The abbot replied, "Shut up and go to your cell." Having received this reply several times and feeling entirely brushed off, finally the novitiate complained, "Father, why will you not help me?" The abbot said, "I have told you, you will draw near to God if you will be silent and still, alone in your room. In the silence your cell will teach you everything you need to know."

Again, this is very similar to the Buddhist notion of emptying as a first and necessary step in a journey of spiritual transformation. There is a Buddhist story about a seeker coming to one of the old masters and asking him to teach him the spiritual path:

Nan-in, a Japanese master during the Meiji era (1868–1912), received a university professor who came to inquire about Zen. Nan-in served tea. He poured his visitor's cup full, and then kept on pouring.

> The professor watched the overflow until he no longer could restrain himself. "It is overfull. No more will go in!" "Like this cup," Nan-in said, "you are full of your own opinions and speculations. How can I show you Zen unless you first empty your cup?"[3]

If we have become spiritually dull, insensitive, and unaware, I suspect that this is not a failure on God's part. If we fill up our lives with entertainment, work, and distractions and even with good things, how will we ever find the spiritual meaning we hoped for in our lives?

We pray not because we want to ask favors from a magical deity in the clouds but because we want to heighten our conscious

3. Reps, *Zen Flesh Zen Bones*, 19.

contact with God and with one another. We pray as an alternative to becoming products of what comes at us through all of the screens we stare into night and day.

By the end of the first century CE, there may have been several versions of "Christianity" in existence, ranging from otherworldly Gnosticism to a kind of political zealotry. I believe that the precursors of the progressive movement could be found in those who were attracted to the dimension of the Jesus message that offered an alternative to the empire, an alternative to warfare, slavery, and service to the aristocracy. Today, to choose what most people are rejecting—to choose a spiritual life and not one of those embarrassingly self-serving magical incantations to keep you out of hell or get you into heaven kinds of religion, but to embrace a rational, intelligent, progressive spirituality—is to trace a spiritual evolution similar to the path of our first-century predecessors. We are choosing not to become the product of advertisements, pornography, or the culture of Hollywood and entertainment; we are rejecting the dominance of the twenty-first-century empire that is a marriage of corporations and governments with their servile institutional priests and pastors.

Our prayer life allows us to empty ourselves of the appetites that drive the commercial empire because capitalism is not our religion. We pray to foster a sense of connection to the universe and to all other people because military power is not our security. We have chosen another way. If we are good enough at it then we will be able to show the world that there is still an alternative. The empire has the money, the media, the military, and the majority, but we are not defeated.

9

What Should We Teach Our Children About Religion?

It happened again that a certain stranger came before Shammai and said to him: "I will become a proselyte providing you teach me the whole Torah while I'm standing on one foot." (Shammai) knocked him down with the builder's rule in his hand. (The stranger) came before Hillel, who made him a proselyte. He told him: --"What is hateful to you do not do to your neighbor. That is the whole Torah. The rest is commentary. Go, learn [it]![1]

—BABYLONIAN TALMUD

MOST SEMESTERS I TEACH a course on Western religions for a local university. The course begins with Zoroastrianism, and from that early Persian influence we talk about the chain of evolution from Persia to the familiar Western religions of Judaism, Christianity, and Islam. I don't expect my students to remember very much about the seemingly exotic rituals and beliefs of Zoroastrianism, but there is a core teaching that I hope will stay with them.

Zoroastrianism teaches that the good life is lived by having three things: right thoughts, right speech, and right actions.[2] I tell my classes that 2500 years of theological evolution have not added

1. Epstein, *Babylonian Talmud*, 31.
2. Ludwig, *Sacred Paths*, 93.

much to those three injunctions, like the story of the first-century rabbi Hillel, who taught a Gentile that the whole of the Jewish faith is summed up in a version of what appears in one form or another in all of the great religions of the world: "What is undesirable to you, don't do to anyone else."

If we were to try to duplicate Hillel's summation, we might say that Buddhism teaches detachment from greed and lust. Islam holds both chastity and charity as core values. Judaism revolves around concepts of justice and mercy. Christianity teaches radical compassion. But one can almost describe this sort of synopsis as being little more than "bumper sticker" spirituality. If we take Hillel's injunction to "go and learn" the rest, just what would that be?

When we ask ourselves, "What is it about our faith that we want to pass on to the next generation?" we realize that it is difficult, without doctrines or creeds to guide us, to clearly articulate a more complicated and comprehensive approach to living a spiritual life. It is difficult, but it must be done and it needs to be expressed in a vehicle that will be utilized in our faith communities.

It was not long after my friends and I started the progressive church where I am the pastor that young parents began to ask, "Do you offer any classes for children?" When you don't have a denomination or a specific religious tradition, finding appropriate religious education materials is more difficult than you might think. We reviewed samples of Sunday school material from the usual suspects: the Unitarian Universalists, the United Church of Christ, the Disciples of Christ, the Presbyterian and Methodist publishing houses, and the Unity movement. What we specifically wanted to avoid was indoctrination into any one sect, and what we found in the literature of what we thought would be kid-friendly denominations was all very obviously designed specifically to indoctrinate.

Denominations are dying. They have outlived their usefulness, and yet, no institution is ever willing to see itself go out of existence without a fight. Each denomination's materials seemed to have the underlying purpose of making sure that the children who grow up in their churches will never leave them—a program that has failed terribly for a couple of generations, but that obvious fact has not yet begun to influence denominational publishing houses.

Thankfully, the Center for Progressive Christianity has made a noteworthy attempt in publishing "A Joyful Path,"[3] a series of Sunday school lessons for elementary students with a focus on behaviors rather than on beliefs. It is not a perfect curriculum for what I'm looking for, but it surely is a step in the right direction.

We want to teach ethics without using either the motivational carrot of heaven or the stick of hell. Without either fear or guilt, without any thought of personal reward, we want to pass along to the next generation a healthy spirituality that can inspire them to grow into what we would call "good people"—though, for me, "good" is always influenced by what Leon Bloy meant when he said that "any Christian who is not a hero is a pig."[4] Progressives are not typically interested in creating Baptists or Episcopalians; we're not even concerned about whether they choose to be Christian, Jewish, Muslim, Hindu, or Buddhist. We want to pass along the values of a healthy spiritual life, whatever that turns out to be for each of them.

We may have a valuable lesson to learn from the churches of the Reformation era, when Catholics were regularly inspired by reading stories about the lives of the saints and Protestants were motivated to courageous action by John Foxe's *Book of Martyrs*. They, of course, promoted the lives of people who died defending their virginity or who died in some act of evangelical zeal, but we should rehearse the lives of our modern saints who gave their lives as modern prophets of justice, tolerance, mercy, and peace.

Our church is adorned with images of people who have led exemplary lives in the modern era: Martin Luther King Jr., Gandhi, Dorothy Day, Archbishop Romero, Black Elk, and Cesar Chavez. Our children should know how Sojourner Truth fought to end slavery and how Dietrich Bonhoeffer stood up to the Nazis. They need to know that even in the darkest days of our history

---

3. Center for Progressive Christianity, "Joyful Path."
4. Schofield, "Musings and Thunderings."

there were thinkers like Henry David Thoreau who were able to articulate a vision for how we could all be changed.

In our day, we are way too interested in tearing down leaders, focusing on their clay feet, in order to make ourselves feel better about ourselves. But for all of the well-known faults of someone like Lyndon Johnson, our children should know how the Voters' Rights Act was passed. They should hear about when our nation, under Johnson, waged war on poverty before we started virtually waging war on the poor through a failed war on drugs and "get tough on crime" political campaigns. We should tell stories about people like Ralph Nader and Howard Zinn who have stood up to speak truth to power.

We should make certain that our children know the stories of modern saints like Martin Luther King Jr. and Nelson Mandela. And we should tell them the truth—not the white-washed versions told now that they are dead. Cities that now have a Martin Luther King highway never invited King to visit their communities and usually did what they could to keep him away. He was investigated and threatened by the FBI, jailed frequently, and held in contempt by many of the people who now speak of him as if they were supportive of him all along.

Nelson Mandela was officially considered to be a terrorist by President Ronald Reagan, who resisted sanctions and divestment from apartheid South Africa. Now, nearly a generation since Mandela was released from the prison where he was tortured and forced into hard labor for twenty-seven years, everyone speaks of him as a modern saint, but we must not forget that what made him important was not just that he led South Africa in a peaceful reconciliation of the races.

He was in prison because he had started a militant opposition to the white government. He was kept in prison only because he refused to renounce violence as a means of overthrowing that government. He was nearly blinded by his twenty-seven years on an island prison where he worked breaking rocks in heat, often over 110°F, but he would not renounce violence because he refused to surrender his human right to fight for freedom.

We did not hear in his recent eulogies that he was a sharp critic of the racism in America and of our invasion of Iraq and Afghanistan, or that he was a friend to Fidel Castro in opposition to American foreign policy.

We should tell our children the truth. The path to being a prophet is not simply a matter of talking about love and forgiveness, even if those are our primary goals.

I believe that Jesus presented a threat to the values and rule of the Roman Empire. That's why they killed him. King was a threat to American apartheid; that's why he was so often beaten and jailed. Mandela was a threat to the economic and civil oppression of the black population of South Africa, and he was thought of as a terrorist before he was thought of as a saint.

Our generation makes heroes out of rock stars and professional athletes but we tend to want to tear down spiritual leaders and political reformers. We need to get over that. My New Testament professor at Vanderbilt, Daniel Patte, enjoined us to "Preach the church to the church." We should tell our own stories of service and prophetic witness to our children.

Our children were born into a world with integrated schools, integrated neighborhoods, and equal opportunity employment. My generation was not born into that world—but some of us made the world change. The children in the congregation where I serve should learn about how that older couple they see on Sunday mornings who now have a hard time walking and hearing, Mel and Ruth Miller, once turned their own home into a miniature United Nations, adopting children of color fifty years ago when doing so meant losing friends, jobs, and personal safety.

Our children who have two mommies or two daddies might assume that this is unremarkable, but many of us marched in the streets and demanded equal rights for their families, and have lost jobs and friends and even suffered vandalism and death threats for doing so. The youth in any congregation should be told and shown how their church serves the poor. We tell our kids and include them when we can in service and sacrifice for the homeless in our city and for the rural poor of Nicaragua. Tell the children in your church that the room where they get refreshments every week is also where members lead meetings on weekdays to help alcoholics and addicts recover their lives.

Forgive me, President Kennedy, but we prefer to both curse the darkness and light candles.[5] Our children will know that we expect great things from them. We want them to be happy and successful. We want their lives to be full of joy and love, but we are not raising them to be a generation of happy consumers. We are raising them to become heroes, and to do that we must show them how it is done.

5. Kennedy, "John F. Kennedy Quotes."

10

What Is So? So What? So?

There are three "so's" I need answered in any research project. "What is so?" "So what?" and "So?" Tell me what the facts are. Tell me why it matters. Tell me what should be done about it.

—DR. TODD SCHAIBLE, CEO OF BURRELL
BEHAVIORAL HEALTH

WHEN I WAS A young pastor serving a church in Louisville, I taught a Wednesday evening Bible class in the church basement for about twenty-five church members. A few miles away, on the same side of town, there was a very popular bar called the Toy Tiger. To boost their Wednesday evening trade, at the same time that I was leading a Bible class, at the Toy Tiger, there was a competition that they called "Naughty Nighty Night."

I would often thank the two-dozen or so members of the church who chose to attend my mid-week class for electing Bible Study over the bar's competition. Just for clarification, one man did ask me, "You don't seriously think that going to the Toy Tiger was actually a viable choice for us, do you?"

Of course, for any of my class members, the drive time would have been about the same. They were all over twenty-one, and any one of them could have made the legal choice to avail themselves of some ribald entertainment if that had been their preference. But for everyone in the room, including myself, our religious world-view did not include such entertainment as a viable option.

Though my theological education had pretty well extinguished any seriously literal view of a divine final judgment in which the fate of my eternal soul would be decided, sending me either into eternal reward or eternal torturous punishment, there still existed a shadow of a lifetime of training to believe that God, like Santa Claus, kept a list of all who had been naughty or nice, so we all inherently knew that we were supposed to be good boys and girls.

We had grown up being indoctrinated into a moral universe in which the boundaries had been drawn by the Lord of the universe from the heavens above. We didn't have to struggle with complicated moral decisions about most things because clear unambiguous lines had been drawn centuries before and written down in a book that we were not allowed to question in any serious way.

On the other hand, progressive religious leaders invite people to lead good lives for the inherent reward of leading a good life, which is a rather vague-sounding invitation to those who have always assumed that the moral universe had solid, concrete boundaries, with heaven on one side and hell on the other. Once the manipulative theological carrot and stick have been taken off the table, we have some serious thinking to do about who we are, who we want to be, and what is right and what is wrong—not because some supernatural theistic God in the clouds told us what is right and what is wrong, but rather because of what is, in and of itself, right or wrong on its own merits.

I introduced this book by talking about evidence-based faith. I'm advocating an approach to religion that is based on what is known and not on what Iron Age myths and superstitions tell us about the world. Physicists sum up the entire universe as being comprised of twelve different types of subatomic particles that are held together by four forces of nature, two of which we can see at work: gravity and the magnetic force. The other two are observable only at the atomic level, and they have the unromantic names of the "strong force" and "weak force." You will never see them anyway, so they don't really need poetic nomenclature, but they basically hold atoms together and make them behave in a way that makes the universe possible.

Accepting this description of reality, we are all made, quite literally, of the stuff that was created in the heart of super-hot stars. The twelve particles of matter and four forces of nature that give us our bodies are the same as the twelve particles of matter and four forces of nature that make up the chair you are sitting on, the bricks in walls around us, the trees, grass, and streams down the road, and the stars and planets in the heavens above us.

As cosmologist Brian Swimme has observed, "Four billion years ago Earth was molten rock. Now it sings opera."[1] We are the product of millions of years of evolution. We are the part of the universe that can now become aware of the existence of the universe and consider its meaning. In fact, I would argue, we create its meaning.

Here is the big shift, the breath-taking, dizzying, sometimes infuriating and frightening shift:

If you grew up as I did, you were taught not to question. You were taught to accept the Bible as the Word of God. You were taught that America is the greatest country in the world. We were led to believe that capitalism was just a part of freedom, democracy, and Christianity, and that we were to defend all of the above with our very lives if necessary and to do so with virtually blind faith and absolute loyalty. And that, dear readers, is the opposite of where we are now.

This old unquestioning approach to life stopped working for most of us. We read our way out of it, thought our way out of it, or were pushed out of it through hardships and heartbreaks. For most of us, it was a combination of all of the above.

Now we understand that to really find meaning we have to question everything. We have not thrown away our sacred scriptures, but we no longer read the Bible as if it were divine legislation. Now we critically examine it. Through science, rational thought,

1. Swimme, *Universe Story*, 21.

and critical thinking, we literally interrogate the universe to find out what is and is not true.

I remember hearing the famous psychiatrist and author, M. Scott Peck, saying that anything we cannot question is an idol, and all idols are slated for destruction. We have protected our religious idols from scrutiny and preserved them into the twenty-first century. But no longer will we reject our gay and lesbian sons and daughters because some ancient nomadic sheepherder condemned homosexuality three thousand years ago and wrote it down in what would become the Bible.

I introduced this chapter with a quote from Dr. Todd Schaible, who is the director of Burrell Behavioral Health in Springfield, Missouri. In 2000, I had applied for and received a grant from Burrell to conduct a research project into methamphetamine use in the Ozarks. Todd called me into his office to talk about the project, and he said to me that there were three essential questions we had to answer: What is so? So what? And, so?

That is, our research needed to discover the facts about what was leading to the rapid increase in use of and addiction to this dangerous drug, and further we needed to be able to articulate clearly why it mattered. We needed to be able to tell the public and the municipal, county, and state governments why they should care. And finally, we needed to do more than just throw facts on the table. Our analysis needed to answer the question, "So what can we do about it?" What is so? So what? And, so?

That conversation has never left me because I have applied it to my life as a pastor, journalist, and college professor. I don't just gather facts as if I were going to print a phone book or contribute to a database. I need to be able to stand up in front a congregation or classroom, or write in a newspaper column or book, and say what is factually true. Then I need to be able to say why it matters. Finally, I need to be able to say what should be done in response to the facts.

If there is a single compelling reason for me to be writing this book about progressive faith, it is to answer the last question, "So?" Many wonderful scholars and writers have described the reasons why we have made this dramatic shift in how we read the Bible, and what we now think about Jesus and other world religions. I am indebted to the disciplined and insightful work of Marcus Borg, John Shelby Spong, John Dominic Crossan, Karen Armstrong, and my own friends and academic peers, Charles Hedrick and David Trobisch, for helping me to understand this very clear and objective approach to what were the protected idols of our faith.

They have done a magnificent job of explaining the origins of the Christian religion in a way that helps us to see what is so. And they have done an admirable job of telling us why it matters. And yet each of them has felt the need, as religious scholars, to rarely speak of that third "So?" They have left it to pastors and practitioners to figure out what is the "So?" of progressive faith.

So, you are backing your car out of the driveway, and you have to make a decision: church or the Toy Tiger? More realistically, once we have been disabused of the superstitious beliefs in a supernatural theistic being who will decide right and wrong, who will send some eternal part of ourselves to either heaven or hell—once we are no longer captured in that intellectual and moral prison—the question becomes: Is life to be lived for personal gratification or is there a larger purpose?

If I sit down on a park bench to eat my sandwich and a homeless, hungry stranger sits down next to me, do I devour my sandwich as quickly as possible or do I divide it and share it with the hungry stranger? Nietzsche would tell you that you are weak to even consider sharing your sandwich, or at least that is how Ayn Rand seems to interpret Nietzsche. From my own observation of the way our economy has been run, and the way banks, corporations and, sadly enough, even our government basically make decisions, it looks like the objectivism of Rand's school of self-gratification is being lived out against the alternative view that I would call a spiritual worldview based on a global perspective on ethics.

Scientific thought deals with facts but facts alone cannot determine ethical direction. I've spent years inviting congregants to reject what cannot be known, what has only been presented to religious people as an assertion of truth. There may be angels and demons, a heaven and a hell, there may be souls, ghosts, and spirits, but since we cannot objectively analyze any of these things, I have repeatedly said that it is meaningless to discuss them.

Still, to be fair, I must acknowledge that there is also a truth claim at the foundation point of progressive faith. There is a fundamental moral choice to be made between a life of selfish personal fulfillment, whether you find that at the Toy Tiger or on Wall Street, and a life lived to deliver the greatest good to the largest number of people. The earth that once was primarily molten lava but now can rise up and sing opera, by means of conscious human beings, possesses the potential of experiencing great pain and sorrow, but we also have the potential of experiencing deep joy and meaning. The choice that I make, the choice I hope that others will make, is to answer that "So?" in a way that is not simply to seek personal gratification but is, instead, to direct one's life in a way that provides the greatest good to the largest number of people.

I previously quoted Neil deGrasse Tyson as saying that we are all connected—to each other biologically, to the earth chemically, to the universe atomically. That is a scientific fact, and I am choosing to infuse that fact with spiritual meaning. I will honor my connection to every human being, to the earth, and to the universe by trying to reduce suffering, increase joy, and protect the integrity of life, the earth, and the universe.

Owning my connection to the human race and to the earth we share, I cannot be indifferent about the fact that there are hungry people in the city where I live, even if I am personally over-fed. I cannot be indifferent about the threat of waging war, even if I am far past the age of being personally recruited into any army. The fact that I am employed does not dilute the fact that many are not. Nor does my access to health care afford me the luxury of being indifferent about those who do not receive appropriate care. The fact that my neighborhood is free of toxic wastes, that I have reliably clean drinking water and fresh air, cannot make me indifferent to the poisoning of the soil, water, and air on our shared earth. Being white, male, heterosexual, and American does not excuse me from the need to work for liberation from oppression for persons of color, women, and those of all sexual orientations, races, and nations of the world. And the fact that I am free to choose where I will drive my car today does not deny the fact that there are more than two million Americans in jail or prison right now, many of whom are incarcerated for reasons so wholly indefensible that it is a social crime for us to keep silent about it.

Once Nietzsche was freed from the domination of traditional religion, his choice did not make him the *ubermensch*, the "superman," even if he thought it did. In fact, followed to the logical conclusion of selfishness and self-service, existence has no meaning at all. Nietzsche did not leave the darkness of religious superstition to evolve into a super human; he left it to devolve into what appears to me to be a kind of existential meaninglessness.

The real *ubermensch*, the real heroes of postmodern existence, are those who choose to take their liberty in hand and to live lives of self-sacrificing service, kicking at the darkness until it surrenders to the dawn of a new light of intellectual honesty.

11

What Answers Does Progressive Faith Offer to the Big Questions?

In music, one does not make the end of the composition the point of the composition. If that were so the best conductors would be those that played the fastest and there would be composers who wrote only Finales . . . it is a hoax, a dreadful hoax. They made you miss everything. We thought of life by analogy with a journey, with a pilgrimage, which had a serious purpose at the end and we were supposed to get to that end, and the thing is to get to that end, success or whatever it is, or maybe heaven after you're dead. But we miss the point the whole way along. It was a musical thing and you were supposed to sing or to dance while the music was being played.[1]

—ALAN WATTS

A GENTLEMAN IN FLORIDA wrote to me to ask, "I am elderly, how can I die peacefully without doctors, bright lights, and terrifying inner anxiety?" Progressives are in the business of reimagining what it means to be a spiritual person in a postmodern, scientific, information-centered world, a world in which children continue to be born, couples get married—or at least they want to, where the law allows—and people still get sick and die.

---

1. Watts, "Music and Life."

The church has historically been the gateway to life's transitions. We bless or baptize infants, confirm or baptize young people who are coming of age, and we perform the rituals around marriage and death. And as the traditional gatekeepers of these events, pastors are usually a part of people's preparations for marriage or for death, both during times of crisis and times of great joy.

For most of modern history, the church and its clergy have offered pretty standard and predictable answers to life's big questions. A great deal of that has been marked with humiliating hypocrisy. The traditional church threatened even little children with the fires of hell unless they believed and behaved in just the right way. Yet, promised the family of virtually every deceased person that heaven awaited their departed family member no matter what kind of moral monster he or she might really have been.

We have allowed only persons of the opposite sex to be united in holy matrimony and told them that they are to remain together, under all circumstances, until they are parted by death. It is as if the Lord God Almighty had some kind of sick pleasure in seeing people remain for their entire lives in meaningless or even abusive relationships. I have felt nausea while standing in the chancel of a church asking people who are too young to know what they want to declare as their major in college to make a pledge to a living arrangement that cannot be questioned for the rest of their lives. You only have to see what they have selected to have tattooed on very visible parts of their bodies to realize that they are not mature enough to make permanent decisions!

We have, for centuries, held out the ephemeral promise of eternity in heaven, and people have taken what solace they could from pretending to believe it while doing everything possible to avoid having to test the hypothesis by actually dying. Among the modern proverbs that I would have engraved in granite along the entry walls of our church is this fundamental truth about progressive faith: We have exchanged false certainty for honest uncertainty.

Sure, traditional religion had a clear and firm answer to most of life's questions. The only problem is that we now realize that none of those answers were right, or at least the answers proffered by traditional religion cannot be known with certainty. With great faith and conviction, ancient Egyptian kings had their bodies prepared so that their physical remains would be revived in the next world. Thousands of years later their expertly preserved bodies are on display in museums all over the globe. Neither their faith nor their magic worked.

There may be life after death, but if there is such an afterlife, no one knows anything about it. Neither the best speculations of our philosophers nor the personal testimonies of those who claim in clinical death experiences to have seen heaven (and why is it that none of those people ever report having seen hell?) can offer any objective, testable, or repeatable evidence about it. And so, while we cannot resist speculation and even hope when we are in the midst of grief for a deceased loved one, our desire cannot dictate the nature of the universe. Hope is a good thing. Self-deception is not, however, the mission of the church.

I attended the funeral of a teenaged girl who was the granddaughter of a friend. The girl and some other underage friends had taken a car joy riding in the country. None of them having a license or driving experience, the end of their excursion was tragic and fatal for this one young woman. The family had no warning, no opportunity even to prepare for the horrifying news of the girl's death. The pastor who conducted the memorial was from a generally progressive denomination, but she stood before the grieving family and confidently announced, "We do not grieve today, because this young woman we have all loved is now enjoying a much better life in a much better place."

This is religious denial at its most heinously dishonest. It not only denies all known reality, it also denies the family their sacred right to grieve. Some things in life are sad, and we should not deny anyone their right to a full-throated expression of their loss, their grief, and the anguish of their souls. Grief is the logical reaction to a life cut short by untimely death. What possible benefit is it for us to make the claim that the universe always balances the scales and makes every bad thing acceptable? In choosing honest uncertainty over false certainty, we do not complicate the horrible losses in life with the guilt of trying, but always at least partially failing, to make ourselves believe that we should not be sad lest we appear to be doubting God.

Progressive faith is devoted to intellectual honesty and a search for spiritual meaning. It is not our goal to take away religious comfort, but to focus on the comfort of meaningful existence. As one modern proverb says, "Don't be afraid your life will end; be afraid that it will never begin."[2]

Traditional religion either specifically teaches or at least emphatically implies that the whole reason for existing is to attain to eternal reward and to avoid eternal punishment. The philosopher Alan Watts challenges that view with the simple observation that we do not sing a song in order to come to its end.

By over-emphasizing the afterlife, we devalue life itself. Telling young couples that there is an implied ultimate goal to marriage, which is to avoid getting divorced at all costs, undermines the value of a day-to-day shared life.

Watts specifically bemoans the message we send to our young people that implies that the goal of education is graduation. There is the implication that you get a degree so that you can get a better job because, somehow, happiness is found in career success. This, Watts flatly says, is a hoax and a terrible one at that.

As a professor, I get to stand in front of a room full of students who have come to study the subject that I have found to be so very interesting that I have devoted my life to the study of it. Even after two decades of teaching, I still engage in the fantasy that this semester I am going to encounter students who will share my enthusiasm for the study of religion and ethics. Too often, however, I encounter young adults who have bought into the hoax. What they often want from me is three hours of college credit with a good grade for the least amount of bother possible.

I wish that I could award each student an "A" on the first day of class and then spend the rest of the semester actually engaged in active learning, though I fear that I might end up spending a lot of time alone, and I'm nearly certain that my university would cease

2. Hansen, "Grace Hansen Quotes."

assigning me classes. What Watts is trying to say to college students, and to the rest of us by extension, is that we should live life to its fullest and find both meaning and joy in it as we go. We do not live our lives so that we may arrive safely at the grave. The late journalist Hunter Thompson said it quite eloquently: "Life should not be a journey to the grave with the intention of arriving safely in a pretty and well preserved body, but rather to skid in broadside in a cloud of smoke, thoroughly used up."[3]

Indeed, the only real answer to the reality of our mortality is to live as meaningfully as possible so that we may come to the time of our death as peacefully as possible. This is not, however, only a matter of choosing reality over superstition. It is also a choice of the present moment over anxiously living for an unknown future.

Paradoxically, Buddhism teaches detachment while acknowledging that everything is connected. That is, human beings are a part of the universe, and we are connected to every living thing and to every part of humanity, but suffering, anxiety, and anguish comes from wanting to own, to hold onto, anything or even to our own existence. The mortality rate is 100 percent, and as threatening as that reality can be, as soon as we accept it death ceases to have so much power over us.

Should I ever marry again, I will hope that it is a relationship that will remain meaningfully intact as long as we both shall live. I would certainly work and sacrifice to do my part to make that come true. I would not, however, remain in an unhealthy relationship beyond the point of reasonable hope for it to become healthy, just to avoid religious guilt or the public shame of a failed marriage. Religious condemnation is almost always neurotic. We need to celebrate love and promote healthy relationships, not forge chains to keep people in misery or abuse.

As I have grown older, my doctor tries to push me into ever more frequent and expensive medical tests to make sure that I do not have some undetected threat to my longevity. I try to be a good patient and cooperate within reason, but I recently assured him, "I am not afraid of death." My physician is an evangelical and the son

---

3. Thompson, "Hunter S. Thompson Quotes."

of an evangelical pastor. He looked at me and with an expression of shock and said, "I never hear that. Most of my patients are in their 80s and they want me to do everything possible to make sure that they do not die. I never hear from any of them that they are not afraid of death." I think that is sad.

I could protect myself from exposure to the possibility of divorce by never allowing myself to fall in love again, but that seems like a very bad way to approach human relationships. Life is a gift. Why would we squander the years of our lives trying to find some divine life insurance that would promise us eternal resuscitation but never be able to put that product up for examination?

As odd as what I am saying may appear in the eyes of traditional Christians, it is neither a new insight nor in any way unique to modern thinkers. Among the most ancient of our shared Scriptures are the musings of the philosopher who wrote Ecclesiastes. In chapter 8, the teacher advises:

> No one has power over the wind to restrain the wind, or power over the day of death; . . . So I commend enjoyment, for there is nothing better for people under the sun than to eat, and drink, and enjoy themselves, for this will go with them in their toil through the days of life that God gives them under the sun. (8:8, 15)

I always felt that my very puritan mother was suspicious of anything that might make one happy. Her religion taught her to live in absolute rejection of all forms of pleasure in order to gain a place in heaven. I think that is a bad bet.

Buddhist monks practice keeping a smile on their faces as a gift that they give to the world. Even when discussing very serious things, they attempt, as an offering to others, to maintain a very cheery appearance, which, frankly, can deny even death the ability to extort misery out of us ahead of its time. I think that the writer of Ecclesiastes is right. We will die one day, and we cannot change that fact. So between now and then we should attempt to do what we can to make the world a better place, adding meaning to every day we have, and we should dance our way through the living of our lives, not rushing to the end of the song.

This is not a matter of denial; rather, it is a matter of defiance. We will not let mortality rob us of life while we are still living, nor will we allow the prospect of personal failure to keep us from throwing our arms open to the potential of love, joy, and success.

The most popular early teacher of Buddhism in the United States was the very colorful monk, Trungpa Rinpoche. I will end this chapter quoting what he often demanded of his American audiences: "You cheer up. You cheer up right now."[4]

---

4. Paine, *Re-Enchantment*, 92.

12

Holy Water, Sacred Land

We abuse land because we regard it as a commodity belonging to us. When we see land as a community to which we belong, we may begin to use it with love and respect.[1]

—ALDO LEOPOLD, EARLY TWENTIETH-CENTURY ENVIRONMENTALIST

For 200 years we've been conquering Nature. Now we're beating it to death.[2]

—TOM MCMILLAN, CANADA'S ENVIRONMENT MINISTER

A TALL, BEAUTIFUL MODEL strides confidently across our TV screens assuring us that coal is our friend, providing both abundant energy, and economically important jobs for Americans. Is she trying to persuade us to rush down to the mall and buy some coal? No, but the apparent motivation for such campaign advertisements is not always the only one. "Clean coal," which is different from coal only because you say "clean", is a myth that the coal industry wants to sell to the voting public so that environmental

---

1. Leopold, *Sand County Almanac*, 4.
2. McMillan, "For 200 Years We've Been Conquering Nature."

concerns about the impact of coal on our water, air, and global temperatures will not interfere with their profits.

But more than that, buying advertisement from corporate media is a way of protecting a vulnerable industry from unfavorable news coverage. In the same way, hospitals run PR campaigns advertising the services of their physicians when most of us have little choice in which cancer center or emergency room we can use. We typically use the one that is in our insurance provider group. So when hospitals buy up large blocks of print and broadcast advertising, they are trying to protect themselves from investigative reporting. When was the last time you saw a newspaper really digging into abusive business practices or medical malpractice at a local hospital?

In some instances, where the disaster is bigger than mere bribes can manage, governments have been known to step in and silence the media rather than depending on the uncertainty of trying to buy influence. More than a year after the damaged reactor in Fukushima, Japan, began leaking radiation into the adjoining ocean water, the government passed a law preventing any coverage of the environmental risks. The law carries a potential of ten years in prison for any journalist who actually does what we depend upon journalists to do.[3] It is understandable that the government has an interest in avoiding public panic, but repressing important and possibly life-saving information is shameful at best, and it is more likely a kind of governmental malfeasance.

Similarly, in North Carolina and Virginia state legislators have refused to fund research into anything related to global warming or rising sea levels, as if refusing to address the science related to what is happening to their shores will somehow keep it from happening.[4] After Hurricane Sandy, the largest and most devastating storm in America's history, hit New Jersey, that state's Republican governor, Chris Christy, began to show a great deal more respect for the more fact-based conversation about how

3. Washington's Blog, "Japan Reacts to Fukushima."
4. Lee, "Update."

human dependence on fossil fuels is pushing our planet towards a dangerous tipping point of climate disaster.

Major world religions have had a hard time getting a handle on the topic of environmental ethics. There are a number of important explanations for our past failure; all of these reasons are barriers that must be overcome: First, Western religions have been very text oriented, seeking authoritative direction from their scriptures, all of which were written in a time when the balance of power between the earth and humans was decidedly on the side of nature. While we find examples of cherishing life, discovering awe in nature, and declarations that certain rivers or places were uniquely holy, there is much more about domination of the earth and fear of nature in all of our ancient scriptures.

Progressives must get past this devotion to ancient religious literature. We do not, for example, have to find a way to interpret the Genesis creation story to create an environmental urgency. Neither do we have to play fast and loose with history, making exaggerated truth claims about either Native American or Druid spirituality, to pretend that we will find substantive direction from these or any other ancient sources.

The motivation for trying to make the Genesis account a demand from God to care for the planet is, at one level, laudable, but doing so requires abandoning our efforts at moving away from supernatural theism and the assumption that God somehow wrote the Bible. You can certainly find examples of a more respectful approach to creation in some primitive religion sources, but you can also find contradictions that would only foster more debate about issues that are, substantively, beyond debate in the real world.

The modern world is in a present crisis not foreseen by ancient prophets or in ancient texts. Now is a time when we must apply our devotion to both ethics and truth to join the moral will of the faith community to the information provided by environmental scientists.

Second, we have at times associated our religion with too specific pieces of land or rivers. Poets often express more urgent truths than do our holy scriptures. I love the line in Michael

Franti's song "Hello, Bonjour" where the poet boldly states that every part of our land, air, and water should be considered holy.[5] Again, the Jewish claim of a Promised Land, the Christian identity with holy sites, the Hindu attribution of holy status to one river, and the Muslim claim to traditional governance of specific nations and holy sites undermines the larger issue that there is nothing about Jerusalem that is more holy than Lexington, Kentucky, or more sacred about Mecca than can be found in Belize City. The Florida swamp is a part of the same earth as the Grand Canyon or the Alps.

Our reverence for one place or body of water should not be determined by tradition, or what we may have believed happened there in our own faith history. We are a part of the earth, and all of the parts of the earth are connected to one another.

There has been too much emphasis placed on a belief in an afterlife that can devalue the only world we actually know exists and whose continued existence we are now threatening. Even for those who feel the need to hold on to belief in an afterlife, I would offer the corrective of Søren Kierkegaard, who cautioned that there are things that are true when they are whispered that become false when they are shouted.[6] Belief in heaven may bring comfort to the dying and solace to the grieving, but this belief has been used to dismiss efforts at saving this world because, as some legislators have asserted, God is in charge of the world and nothing will happen to it without God's approval.

From my perspective, the spiritual passion to protect our planet is threefold. The first is simply a reverence and awe for creation in all of its wonder and beauty. Henry David Thoreau was not the first to find more of the divine in nature than in church, and he will not be the last. One should not preclude the other, but they should certainly be partners in inspiring and educating the spirit of both.

Also, environmental issues have a huge social justice concern. Many of the major sources of pollution are profit-driven industries

5. Franti, "Hello, Bonjour," *Yell Fire!* (ANTI-, 2006).

6. Escamilla, *True When Whispered.*

that are choosing short-term gain over long-term environmental health. The poor of every nation generally wind up living in the areas where these industries dispose of their harmful byproducts. As we saw in the 2004 tsunami in Southeast Asia, when the rising sea level and stronger storm surges send a wall of water onto shore, in most countries it is the poor who are living there in very poorly constructed homes who are the most vulnerable. The resources of the earth should not be the sole possession of those who have manipulated governments and banking interests into giving them exploitative rights that are, in any rational analysis, not the right of any individual or narrow interest. We can innately understand that the air belongs to all of us, but it would be helpful if we could maintain some of that sense of global connection when it comes to real estate.

Finally, this is a matter of compassion for future generations. The present generation that stands on the face of the earth does not have a right to use up the resources of the earth that will shortly be inherited by future generations. We talk about owning land as a part of our economic and personal safety interests, but how can any mortal own something that lasts forever? We are stewards of the land and as stewards we have a much more vital interest that trumps our desire for personal profit. This should go without being said. What could be more obvious than the fact that we must leave behind a planet that can be successfully inhabited by future generations? Still, sometimes the most obvious truths are the ones the faith community should repeat the most often and the most loudly.

It would not be difficult to become exhausted with the virtual panic in the voices of many environmental advocates. However, we should not fail to note that when we have become convinced that it needed to be done, we have been able to reverse the trends of planetary degradation. We have been able to restore forests and clean up rivers and lakes. We even, through individual effort and changes in governmental policies, reversed the erosion of the ozone layer of our atmosphere—even though no one goes camping in the ozone layer or posts vacation pictures from there on their Facebook page.

People can, when given the correct information and the reason to act on it, stop poisoning their own habitat. Environmentalists often look more like Michael Moore than like that lady who keeps telling us that we should have more coal in our breakfast cereal because mercury poisoning isn't all that bad! But we must first choose not to be either gullible or fatalistic.

Understanding how to care for the earth is complicated, and it takes an investment of personal energy. At many junctures, personal sacrifice will be necessary to make the needed changes in our use of the earth.

The largest consumption of fossil fuels is expended in two arenas, the heating and cooling of our homes and transportation, so this is where we must concentrate our efforts. It would be wonderful if we were all motivated to do the right thing because it is the right thing to do; however, human nature being what it is, doing the right thing is always a bit easier if it saves us some money at the same time. Strengthening our conscience and protecting our financial resources are not always mutually exclusive.

Learning to recycle, to refrain from using disposable items, to insulate our homes, and to be more cautious about the use of energy with our appliances, lights, and television, as well as heating and cooling can lower our bills while acting to save the planet. Investing in energy-efficient light bulbs, water heaters, and appliances have upfront costs but they promise long-term savings. Stephen Chu, the Obama Administration's Energy Secretary, has been trying to get the message out that something as simple as using white shingles on our homes could cut our air conditioning bills by 20 percent.[7] So, why is it even possible to buy dark colored shingles? Why do we continue to show indifference about huge matters of environmental integrity only to serve venial matters of esthetics? While nations such as Germany are covering most newly constructed houses with solar panels, we're still wasting space and energy on dark brown shingles!

7. Barringer, "White Roofs."

Transportation is a larger and more complex issue. Larger, more powerful vehicles are attractive to us for comfort, safety, utility, and for reliability in inclement weather. However, choosing smaller, hybrid, or alternative-energy transportation is an option for most of us, and it is something we can do proactively to help conserve limited resources and to cut back on pollution. Still, a huge percentage of the consumption of gasoline in major cities is used by drivers who are looking for parking places. All of us have experienced sitting for long periods of time in traffic jams where there are rows and rows of cars, stopped in multiple lanes as far as the eye can see, all burning fuel while waiting to move.

The creation of an energy-efficient mass transit system would require a sea change in priorities for nations such as ours. We are not only accustomed to private transportation, but our economy is deeply invested in the manufacture, sales, and maintenance of automobiles and all of the accompanying road construction. Both government and private corporate interests will continue to use their influence to keep Americans in cars.

Mass transit could cut down on pollution, consumption of fossil fuels, traffic accidents, the amount of land taken up in parking, personally owned garage space, and the time it takes to move from one place to another. There certainly would be a huge upfront investment to build this kind of infrastructure, but that is a small concern compared to the hurdle of persuading Americans to want mass transit rather than bigger cars and more highways.

The technology exists. Other nations have taken great strides in this direction. All that stands between us and making huge progress in protecting both our environment and our personal incomes is the collective will to change.

The most important task of the ancient prophets, of the early church, and of any meaningful incarnation of the church in the future, is to speak truth to power. Our news media is almost exclusively corporation owned and profit driven. Even our public media is influenced by government grants and corporate sponsorship. The church must maintain its independence from profit-driven interests and find the courage to be faithful to the truth in the face of changing public opinions.

Pastors are not environmental experts, but we surely do need to expose ourselves to the research and insights of the people who do have expertise in this arena. We need to articulate a passionate, informed, and prophetic message to a public that may not hear the imperative truth about our ecology anywhere else.

One of my favorite old hymns, as previously mentioned, is "Once to Every Man [*sic*] and Nation." In it there is a line that says, "Truth forever on the scaffold, wrong forever on the throne, yet that scaffold sways the future." I fear that too much of the mainstream church is cowering in a self-defensive posture, trying to hold on to its meager existence for another generation. What I am trying to say about being bold in the area of environmental activism is what William Shedd meant when he said, "A ship in harbor is safe but that is not what ships are for."[8] The church exists for telling the truth and, given the crisis that is at hand in the environment, it is past time that we stop being afraid of the consequences of being prophetic, because the consequences of silent consent are surely much worse!

8. Shedd, "William Shedd Quotes."

13

Just War Theory in a Nuclear World

So, yes, I came to a conclusion that war cannot be tolerated, no matter what we're told. And if we think that there are good wars and that, therefore, well, maybe this is a good war, I wanted to examine the so-called good wars, the holy wars, and—yeah, and take a good look at them and think again about the phenomenon of war and come to the conclusion, well, yes, war cannot be tolerated, no matter what we're told, no matter what tyrant exists, what border has been crossed, what aggression has taken place. It's not that we're going to be passive in the face of tyranny or aggression, no, but we'll find ways other than war to deal with whatever problems we have, because war is inevitably—inevitably—the indiscriminant massive killing of huge numbers of people. And children are a good part of those people. Every war is a war against children.

So it's not just getting rid of Saddam Hussein, if we think about it. Well, we got rid of Saddam Hussein. In the course of it, we killed huge numbers of people who had been victims of Saddam Hussein. When you fight a war against a tyrant, who do you kill? You kill the victims of the tyrant. Anyway, all this - all this was simply to make us think again about war and to think, you know, we're at war now, right? In Iraq, in Afghanistan and sort of in Pakistan, since we're sending rockets over there and killing innocent people in Pakistan. And so, we should not accept that.

Progressive Faith and Practice

> We should look for a peace movement to join. Really, look for some peace organization to join. It will look small at first, and pitiful and helpless, but that's how movements start.[1]
>
> —HOWARD ZINN

IN THE 1997 FILM *Good Will Hunting*, Matt Damon plays a young genius named Will Hunting who works as a janitor at MIT. At one point he is required to see a therapist, played by Robin Williams, who sees Will's huge potential. Hunting suggests to his therapist that he read Howard Zinn's *A People's History of the United States* to get the truth about America.

Damon's character may have only read Zinn, but Damon himself actually grew up living next door to the famous historian and even volunteered to be the voice on the audio version of the book. I have met a lot of famous people in my life, but I especially treasure the memory of hearing Zinn in person, first at Missouri State University, then at Drury University, and finally at Harvard, where I had the chance to meet him.

When my friends and I started Community Christian Church in 2008, the first group study we did was on Zinn's book. We spent nearly a year discussing it because we wanted to ground our shared life in the painful reality of the nation we have inherited.

The progressive movement doesn't really have a canon of saints, but if we ever do, I want to place the late Howard Zinn's name in nomination. If, as I have suggested, the mission of the church is to speak truth to power, Zinn is certainly one of the best modern examples of doing just that.

I have been saying that there are four primary arenas of concern for the progressive church in the twenty-first century. The first is poverty and social justice. The second is related to ending racism and prejudice. The third is a renewed concern for caring for the environment. The fourth has to do with advocating for peaceful resolutions of international problems and working to avoid war.

1. From a speech at Boston University on November 11, 2009. Zinn, "Three Holy Wars."

These four have many overlapping dimensions; in fact one often feeds the intensity of the other. Racism or prejudice may not be the provocation for a government to declare war on a neighbor, but it has certainly been used to fuel the passion of armies. Preventing new wars implies the conduct of international relationships in a way that makes peace possible. There is an old Turkish proverb that says, "A hungry person is an angry person." The eradication of poverty fosters international peace. A sane, sustainable, and just use of natural resources also promotes social justice and international harmony.

For centuries any religious conversation about a just cause for war begins with the thinking of St. Augustine as formalized by St. Thomas Aquinas. It is unfair to try to condense the thought of either of these two giants of church history, but for the sake of brevity I will summarize their justification for war to these three points:

1. A war must be waged as a last resort and only by a sovereign nation.

2. A war must have a just provocation and not be motivated by the prospect of gaining profit or power.

3. A war must be fought with a reasonable expectation of success, and it must end in peace.

In almost every instance, governments try to sell their populations on the perception that the war they are proposing has met all or most of these criteria. Perhaps even more than our international peers, Americans posture ourselves as either acting in self-defense or carrying out a police action that stops the abuses of a tyrant. The particular genius of Howard Zinn is in taking a serious historical look at those claims and helping us to see how we have been lied to and manipulated in almost every case.

In his last major address, quoted above, Zinn talks about the use of the belief in a kind of "holy war" to gain public approval or at least acquiescence to our modern military adventures. He describes the American Revolutionary War, the Civil War, and

WWII as our "holy wars" whose virtue is seen to be beyond question. And then he goes on to question the historical memory of each.

We then use those "holy wars" to justify subsequent wars by comparing, for example, the Nicaraguan Contras to the freedom-loving Revolutionary War soldiers of our history, or comparing Saddam Hussein or Manuel Noriega to Adolph Hitler. It is quite a fall from grace to have been on the CIA's payroll at one time to then becoming someone often compared to Hitler, but it was not only Hussein and Noriega who were once on the American payroll; even Osama Bin Laden received American support through the aid we gave to the Mujahedeen during their war with the Soviet Union. Our military adventurism has often found us with strange bedfellows.

Zinn points out that, yes, the Revolutionary War gave us independence from Great Britain, but challenges whether that war was really about equality, freedom, and independence. It wasn't for the black slaves, indentured servants, women, or the landless poor. No matter what high-sounding ideals were articulated in the Declaration of Independence and the Constitution, these documents were used to establish a white male aristocracy in the former British colonies.

And yes, slavery was ended by the Civil War, but was that war really fought to give American blacks liberty and equality? Did they get liberty and equality at the end of the war . . . or a generation later . . . or two, three, or four generations later?

World War II did end with the defeat of fascism. So, do we believe that fascism is now defeated? Even our most defensible wars have a much more tarnished halo than we like to believe. You have been told that we dropped atomic bombs on Japan to avoid the greater casualties we would have experienced by having to invade Japan. There are substantial historical reasons to doubt the validity of that claim. We had killed 100,000 Japanese in Tokyo with conventional bombs just before dropping the atomic bombs. No one ever talks about that, and I suspect that most Americans don't know of it.

Japan was defeated and many believe that they were ready to surrender before we dropped those atomic bombs. I find it entirely plausible to assume that we dropped them to show the Soviets that we had this terrible weapon and that we had the will to use it. Do you believe that everyone in Hiroshima was an enemy to freedom and liberty?

We killed 600,000 Germans with conventional bombs, 100,000 of who died in a single night in Dresden. Were all of the residents of Dresden Nazis—the women, children, and the elderly? We like to think of ourselves as liberators, defenders of justice— we want to be that "city on a hill"—but, in an approximation of the wise words of Yoda, it is a very rare thing when wars make a nation great.[2]

At the time the United States launched a war against Iraq, a majority of Americans had either been tricked by government propaganda or had tricked themselves into believing that Iraq was responsible for the 9/11 attack on the United States. There was no connection, of course, nor were our weapons inspectors mistaken in their repeated attempts at telling the Bush Administration that there were no WMDs hidden in Iraq. It is true enough that Saddam Hussein was a bad guy, but any kind of intellectual honesty compels us to acknowledge that he wasn't killing Iraqis at the rate that we did during a decade of war and occupation, nor can we claim to have, on average, much improved the circumstances of the average Iraqi citizen.

Early in 2014, Curtis Reeves, a seventy-one-year-old retired policeman, shot and killed Chad Oulson in a Florida movie theater because Chad wouldn't stop texting during the movie. We know how annoying it is to be sitting beside someone in a theater or classroom or in church who is staring at his or her phone and texting, but whatever punishment may be appropriate for this annoyance, we're all pretty clear that lethal shooting is an insanely over-the-top reaction.[3] Somehow, we are not able to be similarly

---

2. "Wars not make one great." Star Wars Blog, "StarWars.com 10."
3. Botelho, "Witnesses of Florida Theater Killing."

clear about when our use of military force is an insanely out-of-bounds response to provocation.

On September 10, 2001, there were "What Would Jesus Do?" rubber bracelets being sold on the counters of book stores and gas stations all over my hometown. In an entirely uncoordinated but massively hypocritical gesture, every one of those bracelets disappeared on 9/11 because no one wanted to ask that question anymore; nor would they tolerate any corollary questions like, "Who would Jesus bomb?" The apparently desirable piety implied in the question became increasingly unwelcome in a country that wanted revenge in the bloodiest way possible.

The moral problem for Americans was that we were not attacked by a nation. If any country could actually have been reasonably blamed it would be Saudi Arabia, but its government was not directly responsible. What follows is the musing of a parish pastor, not a trained military strategist, but it seems to me that any reasonable military response to 9/11 would have been police action going after terror cells and training camps.

I said at the time of the build up to war in Afghanistan, and I have often repeated since then, that our wars in Afghanistan and Iraq were not wars on terrorism but wars of economic opportunity. The waging of war makes the manufacturers of military hardware and the suppliers of support material to the armed forces very rich. The flow of taxpayer money to military industrial corporations slows down when there is not a hot war or at least the threat of one.

Among the armed forces there are thousands of examples of individual and unit courage, valor, genius, and sacrifice on the battlefield. Still, no one should ever fall prey to the ruse that admiration for the contribution of any individual soldier must also necessitate supporting the politicians who made the decision to put that soldier in harm's way. Those are two entirely different issues.

You will be told that if you support the troops that you must not question the war. That is a logical fallacy of the first order. Sure, if I lost a loved one on the battlefield or if I had lost my legs or my sanity on foreign soil then I would want to believe that this sacrifice was made in the cause of defending freedom. Who wouldn't want his or her sacrifice honored with such accolades? But what we want doesn't change the facts.

The inconvenient truth is that most wars are an economic scam. Wars transfer wealth into the hands of the very wealthy and powerful but accomplish little else. In the case of the invasion of Iraq, we were told that the proceeds from the oil fields of Iraq would finance our military action there, but that was never really the plan. Already, nearly $200 billion in contracts have been given by our government to the corporations that are involved in Iraq, with the largest winner being Dick Cheney's former employer, Halliburton, and it's subsidiaries.[4] Some very sober estimates place the actual eventual costs of these two wars between $4 and $6 trillion.[5]

Consider other ways such resources might have been spent. For example, America's entire student loan debt is estimated to be just over $1 trillion. How would it have affected life in America if we forgave all existing student debt and made all colleges and universities tuition-free for a decade? When we consider the costs of war we have to think about what we are not doing so that we can devote resources to foreign wars, and the contrast rarely makes war seem like a good investment.

Did America, with this huge expenditure of human life and financial and natural resources, bring an end to the threat of terrorism? Again, in any honest estimate, we not only did not put a dent in terrorism but have succeeded in aggravating the problem and virtually assuring ourselves of future terrorist strikes for the rest of our natural lives. There is no expert on the consequences of war that I respect more than the brave young Pakistani woman Malala Yousafzai, who survived an assassination attempt by a Taliban extremist. Though seriously injured by a gunshot wound to the head, she fought her way back to health following many surgeries and a long recovery. In a late 2013 conversation with President Obama, this sixteen-year-old "schooled" the American president in how drone strikes in her country fuel terrorism rather

4. Young, "And the Winner."
5. UPI, "Harvard Study."

than preventing terrorism.[6] Such a conclusion should be obvious to any thoughtful observer, but that insight has not yet penetrated into the halls of power.

Probably every peace advocate in the world knows by heart the warnings given by President Eisenhower against the threat of our own military industrial complex. Most of the time, people mistakenly put together pieces of two speeches delivered by the five-star general who would later become president of the United States.

Shortly after Eisenhower took office in his first term as president, Joseph Stalin died. It was then that he delivered a speech about the prospects for world peace in which he said:

> Every gun that is made, every warship launched, every rocket fired signifies, in the final sense, a theft from those who hunger and are not fed, those who are cold and are not clothed. This world in arms is not spending money alone. It is spending the sweat of its laborers, the genius of its scientists, the hopes of its children. The cost of one modern heavy bomber is this: a modern brick school in more than 30 cities. It is two electric power plants, each serving a town of 60,000 population. It is two fine, fully equipped hospitals. It is some fifty miles of concrete pavement. We pay for a single fighter with a half-million bushels of wheat. We pay for a single destroyer with new homes that could have housed more than 8,000 people.[7]

Eisenhower was no idealistic peacenik. He was not advocating disarmament or pacifism. But he was pointing out that every dollar we spend on military hardware keeps us from spending that dollar on food, medicine, education, or housing.

It was eight years later that President Eisenhower shocked the world by delivering a farewell speech that concentrated on warning against the irrational military spending of a coalition between Congress and the corporations that build military hardware. He saw this threat growing larger during his presidency as the Cold

6. Mirkson, "Someone Finally Asked Malala."
7. Schlesinger, "Origins of That Eisenhower."

War sent military spending through the roof. He saw it, but he failed to stop it. Since Eisenhower, Republican and Democratic presidents have both found themselves incapable of reasonably curtailing the power of a Congress that is controlled by military industrial interests.

Where has the church been in the midst of all of this? Who are our prophets? There have been a few, and some of them were absolutely of biblical stature—especially Dorothy Day and Daniel Berrigan come to mind. But for the most part the church in the United States has been as much of a silent partner to immoral and illegal wars as were the churches of Italy and Germany during WWII. Ironically, this has seemed to be truer during the Persian Gulf wars than even during the Vietnam War era. As Thomas Jefferson famously said, "In every country and in every age, the priest has been hostile to liberty. He is always in alliance with the despot, abetting his abuses in return for protection of his own."[8]

So here is what I have to say to the progressive church of the twenty-first century: Don't ever play the part of a whore for any despot, tyrant, or lying chief executive ever again. Don't ever play dumb or remain indifferent when someone is trying to sell our nation another war.

Even more importantly, we must ask ourselves what peaceful measures can be taken to avoid the kinds of international hostilities that end up in war. Wars are very rarely ideological in nature. They are almost always economic. Beyond all talk about the threats of radical Islam, communism, socialism, and fascism there is, in fact, a real enemy of the world's people: poverty.

The United States currently deploys an army of around 200,000 people at a cost of between $1 and $2 million per year per soldier, depending upon where they are deployed.[9] We deploy this army to help foster global peace and stability. Let's imagine, just for conversation's sake, that we cut that military deployment by 75 percent by closing all of the bases that were built to fight WWII, pulling back weapons that we will never need, and

8. Jefferson, *Writings*, 119.
9. Wikipedia, "United States Armed Forces."

radically shifting our priorities away from the threat of violence and towards creating stability.

Rather than deploying 200,000 soldiers, we could deploy nearly as many teachers, agricultural specialists, doctors, and engineers. What if we make it our goal to raise the literacy rate of the world to over 90 percent, make safe water and food universally available, provide AIDS medications in Sub-Saharan Africa, and wipe out malaria and polio? It is reasonable to suggest that we could accomplish all of these goals for about one fourth of what we spend on the military, so that we could cut military spending in half, transform the world into a stable and safe place, and still have the strongest military in the world for those instances when only military action can do the job.

There are always people who get very rich off of wars, and so the proposals I have just enumerated would not be popular on Wall Street or Capitol Hill, but if they can't find traction in our churches, synagogues, and mosques then religion really is a fraud. The program I am suggesting of diverting military resources to medicine, education, agriculture, and infrastructure is not only a workable goal that could create global stability and peace in less time than we have had troops in Afghanistan but, frankly, we would have to be crazy not to do it.

14

The Justice System and Our Prison Nation

When a great man like Nelson Mandela passes, it's also common to wonder if we'll ever see his kind again. But there's no doubt that the Nelson Mandelas and Martin Luther Kings and Václav Havels of the 21st century are striding among us. But you can't see it, because if he or she was shaking hands with world leaders and greeted by adoring throngs and serenaded by children's choirs, then they wouldn't be the next true Mandela or King or Havel.

No, the next Nelson Mandela of the world is rotting in a jail cell tonight, just like Mandela nearly withered for 27 years on Robben Island. Or he is on someone's terrorist watch list, or she is segregated and searched every time she travels through an international airport. Somewhere, government spies are reading the emails of the next Nelson Mandela. They are tracking his cell phone and listening to his calls, or monitoring her meetings with their undercover cops.[1]

—WILL BUNCH

FOR THE PAST SEVERAL years there has been a very unusual cross-country bike race in France that is for prison inmates. The "Penal Tour de France"[2] is a program that leaves many Americans scratching their heads. We think of jail time strictly as punishment, like societal revenge for crimes committed. In France, however, they

1. Bunch, "World's Next Mandela."
2. BBC News, "Penal Tour de France."

take a different perspective. They are trying to figure out how to use prison time to help inmates learn how to live productive lives within their society.

We tend to beat down our inmates. We will not allow them to earn degrees or job certifications in prison. We did at one time, but in a "get tough on crime" mentality we do not want to give a prisoner an opportunity not afforded to people who have not been convicted of a crime. One could argue that we should give these opportunities of education to everyone in financial need, but that, evidently, would be deemed as socialism rather than common sense. What could be more logical than using prisoners' time in incarceration to give them an education that will enable them to productively and meaningfully fit into society when they are released? To do that, however, we have to change our thinking from revenge to reform.[3]

If you agree with my insistence that the future of the church is dependent upon our ability to become morally relevant in society, it is quite possible that one of the primary arenas where we must turn our attention is the two million Americans who are currently in jail or prison. This hidden nation of prisoners within our nation may need what religious communities have to offer the most, while being the least likely ever to have contact with us.

Admittedly, the prison system does not make it easy. In the early 1990s, I tried repeatedly to set up college classes in the federal medical prison near my home. Initially, I was told that it would take too much staff time to move prisoners into and out of a classroom. Then, in 1994, Congress changed regulations around the use of federal Pell Grants that made it impossible to find tuition dollars.[4] We could wish that colleges and universities who trumpet their "public affairs" missions would offer credit classes without tuition charges in prisons, but they do not.

I then applied for clearance to teach basic non-credit self-help classes in the local county jail, where some inmates live for more than two years without meaningful programming. The day

3. Fleisher, "US Prisons Don't Fund Education."
4. Troustine, "Battle to Bring Back Pell Grants."

of my first class there was an incident at the jail as I sat in a waiting area preparing to teach. Two new guards had urinated on inmates through a screen in the roof of the gymnasium and the prison officials decided that it would be best not to have outsiders working too closely with convicts.[5] I have suspected that my role as an opinion writer for the local newspaper may have increased the warden's discomfort, because they really needed to keep prisoner abuse out of the media.

Far from the experience of a bicycle race in rural France, prisoners in our penal system experience violence, rape, and deprivations of every sort and are often put into situations where they have to solicit money from family members and friends to pay the extortion charged by other inmates for protection from abuse. Once out of incarceration the humiliations can multiply. With a criminal record, it is very difficult to find employment and yet ex-cons are required to pay fees for their mandatory probation officer visits and follow-up supervision. Some even have to pay back states or communities for the cost of their incarceration.

People on parole are making many of the annoying telemarketing calls we receive because these commission sales jobs are one of the few places where they can find work. As infuriating as these telephone interruptions can be to us, can you imagine what it is like on the other end of the line as people suffer angry verbal abuse all day long?

Not that it is easy to garner sympathy for sex offenders, but we must bear in mind the fact that nearly all sex offenders were once victims themselves. They are the most likely to be violently treated in prison and the most likely to be reviled, unemployed, and homeless once out of prison. Most homeless shelters will not give them even temporary shelter.

Permanently placed on a publicly available sex offender list, they often cannot even live with willing family members or friends because of the reactions of neighbors. Though we cannot afford to be too lax about the threat posed by those who are likely to repeatedly offend, we also have to do something much better than what

5. *USA Today*, "Guard Convicted."

we are doing. If their offenses are not sufficient to merit killing them, then we must find some way to allow them to live!

Because reintegration into society has been made so very difficult, our incarceration recidivism rate is the worst in the world.[6] Every part of this equation should startle the conscience of Americans. We incarcerate a higher percentage of our population than any other country in the world, and yet even so we have the highest recidivism rate, demonstrating that we are also the worst at operating prisons.

This is complicated by the fact that the one thing Americans have been really good at is finding a way to make a profit even in the midst of tragedy. Building prisons and then operating them has become a huge profit source, so much so that some states have started privatizing their prisons so that every night an American is kept in jail is another transfer of money from citizens to corporations. As an illustration of just how profitable this industry is, in 2013 the GEO Group Inc., a for-profit prison corporation, donated $6 million for naming privileges of a football stadium in Florida.[7] You might think that the morally questionable relationship between the state and for-profit prisons would be something you would want the public to know as little about as possible, but Florida Atlantic University in Boca Raton now bears the name of GEO Group on its stadium for all to see. Perhaps, as prophet Jeremiah said of his people, the state of Florida "does not know how to blush" (Jer 8:12).

When for-profit prisons are paid by inmate volume, what possible motivation do they have to try to help prisoners reform and succeed outside of prison? In fact, recidivism fattens their profits and so they will do what they can to prevent education, job training, counseling, and anything that might make a prisoner less likely to come back and bring more tax dollars with them.

Every nation has citizens who are entirely convinced that their own homeland is the greatest country in the world. Americans have not only had a loudly stated conviction that ours is the

6. Ward, "Incarceration."

7. Kirkham, "Florida Atlantic Football Stadium."

greatest nation on the globe, but for much of our history we've had the immigration statistics to back that up.

However, our dramatically growing income disparity and class divisions threaten to destroy any plausible defense of that claim. I will discuss income disparity in the next chapter in greater detail, but there is a direct link between impoverished neighborhoods and their underfunded schools and the growing prison population. This has now been dubbed the "school to prison pipeline."[8]

Beyond the issue of the increasingly impassable gulf between the upper and lower economic classes that now keeps the poor in America forever poor, we have former inmates, the growing subclass in our society for whom there is little opportunity for change and even less social sympathy. We are no longer world leaders in many categories, but in one way we are unrivaled at the top of the list, though shamefully: we have the largest percentage of our population living behind bars. Seven out of every thousand Americans are incarcerated. China, long famous for their government's repression of their own citizens, has an incarceration rate that is less than 20 percent of ours. Vietnam has less than 10 percent as many citizens in jail as we do.[9]

How does this once great nation disown so many of its own sons and daughters? It is, in many ways, a failure of our schools, our economy, our families, and our judicial system. We must also say that it is reflective of a failure of our churches. In the big picture, it is a failure of our society as a whole. There are too many drugs, not enough decent jobs, too much violence, and not nearly enough love. We have too much moral judgment and not enough compassion. We are too committed to revenge-driven punishment and not enough interested in reform and recovery.

The United States is one of the few countries in the world that allows for a huge disparity in education spending based on school districts, allowing affluent areas to have well-funded schools while poor areas have only ill-equipped, underfunded, and understaffed

8. Amurao, "Fact Sheet."
9. Wing, "Here Are All."

schools. Anyone can see that it should be the other way around. The children of the poor need more enrichment in education than their middle- and upper-class peers whose families can well afford the kind of travel and cultural experiences that give their kids a leg up in life.

We have created a broken school system and a for-profit prison system that work together to fast-track kids from poor neighborhoods from school to jail—a tragedy complicated all the more by race. There are five times as many white drug users as there are black drug users, and yet blacks charged with drug offenses are ten times more likely to go to jail. As the prison population has risen by nearly 50 percent over the past three decades, this has disproportionately affected the black community.[10]

Some of that is simple racism but a lot of it is an indication of just how corrupt our judicial system has become. We have prided ourselves on the strength of the belief that our constitutional government creates equality in our society. Our courthouses are adorned with statues depicting the blindfolded Lady Justice. Surely blind justice would not consider race, class, language, sexual orientation, or gender, but our judicial system does not measure up to this high-minded ideal.

Howard Zinn has written often about the inequality of justice among the economic classes in the hands of the judiciary.[11] In my own experience, it seems that our judicial system does not so much decide on who is right and who is wrong as it decides who can pay their lawyers the most. Far too little of our justice system is engaged in the pursuit of justice and much too much of it serves the interests of income for lawyers and profit for corporations.

There is one judicial system for the wealthy, another for the poor, and, in my experience, a third one that legal professionals use for their own issues, giving lawyers a literal court system for their own fraternity and sorority. There could not be, in any Third World country, more personal favors, disappeared tickets, and

---

10. NAACP, "Criminal Justice Fact Sheet."
11. Welch, "Howard Zinn's Critical Criminology."

inexplicably favorable rulings based on kinship and friendship than we have allowed to exist in our court system.

Somehow, over the past half century, the laudable "War on Poverty" evolved into the "War on Drugs." We were making progress in the war on poverty. We don't talk about it often enough, but when President Johnson set out to substantively change the face of poverty in America it was working. But as that movement became focused on drug abuse and all of our resources were devoted to arresting and imprisoning drug users, the earlier progress was lost and we have now done something much more insidious.

Technological advances and the exporting of manufacturing jobs have left us with a surplus in our workforce. We are removing many of the extra laborers from the pool by imprisoning two million of them and leaving millions more with a criminal record that necessarily excludes them from meaningful competition for decent jobs.

It is no exaggeration then to say that our nation is in need of a spiritual revival. Religious people must convincingly teach the message of compassion to our society, which has far too often chosen profit over people. We have continued to pour resources into the complete failure of the war on drugs—resources that could be used to build up schools and fund public infrastructure projects that would pull us meaningfully into the twenty-first century.

Western European countries, which have almost no church attendance compared to the United States, also enjoy an incarceration rate that is less than one-fourth of ours. That hurts. Why would the nation with the most churches also have the most prisons? I cannot help thinking that traditional religion has played a role in teaching people to deny reality, disregard the aspects of our society that are seriously broken by focusing on perfection in an imagined heaven, and distracting us from the real work of loving one another.

The progressive church has a mission to tell the truth, to shine light into the dark places of our world. If we are to be a prophetic church, then we must stand up to things like income inequality, unequal public schools, joblessness, and a senseless devotion to the energy sources, transportation technology, and a foreign policy of war that really became inappropriate for implementation sixty years ago.

We can employ more people by rebuilding our infrastructure, renewing our power grid, building alternative energy production facilities, and increasing mass transit. We can decide to fund our public schools, make it possible for the poor to attend college, and make prisons places of healing and learning rather than places of rape, torture, and training in how to be better criminals.

We can decriminalize addiction and assume that anyone who says that they need a prescription for medical marijuana to cope with how crazy our country has been for the past generation probably deserves to have it and certainly doesn't deserve to be in jail for it.

A society bent on revenge is a sick society. A society intent on healing, forgiveness, compassion, and peace is a nation that can find a plausible reason to call itself the greatest nation in the world.

15

Our Preference for the Poor

Now, it's not as if fiscal scolds really arrived at their position based on statistical evidence. As the old saying goes, they used Reinhart-Rogoff the way a drunk uses a lamppost—for support, not illumination.[1]

—PAUL KRUGMAN

MONEY DOES NOT EXIST. Money is a concept. To illustrate this point, the philosopher Alan Watts used the analogy of a carpenter who came to work one day and was told that they could not finish building the house he was working on because they had run out of inches.[2] A carpenter builds out of lumber but measures the lumber in inches, but inches are not real; inches are a concept. Money is not real. It is a medium used to measure the value of things and to make it easier to trade in objects, labor, energy, and land.

Actual wealth resides in resources such as land, rare metals, energy sources, food, water, building materials, labor, and vehicles. Money is just a concept we have invented to help us to distribute real wealth. Currency only works if we agree on the system and play by the economic rules that create it.

Real wealth is created when we build something, grow something, mine something, or assemble something. Unfortunately, our economic system allows for a great deal of real wealth to be

1. Krugman, "Fiscal Fever Breaks."
2. Watts, *Eastern Wisdom, Modern Life*, 108.

transferred into the hands of people who do not create wealth but simply own assets or control them through financial instruments and institutions. When we have idle workers who are not building, growing, and making things then our total real wealth is going down. The best of economic systems keeps people working in the creation of real wealth.

When the Hebrew prophet Isaiah was speaking poetically of the way the world should be, how it could be if God were in charge, he said about workers that:

> They shall build houses and inhabit them; they shall plant vineyards and eat their fruit. They shall not build and another inhabit; they shall not plant and another eat. (Isa 65:21–22)

The remnant of Israelites living in Babylon had been slaves. They built houses for their masters. They had been gardening to grow crops for their "owners." And their distant memory of their people was the ancient memory of slavery in Egypt and service to Assyria. They longed for justice, and what justice looked like to them was an economic system in which the poor got a share in what they produced.

In ancient times as well as in modern times, there is always some pressure on the economic system to give a smaller and smaller share of the produce to the people who are doing the producing, and a larger and larger share to people who manage the financial institutions, the government, the owners of natural resources and land. From time to time, societies find that they have to restrike a balance between the rich and the poor or their entire society will collapse. This scenario has been seen on every continent in every age of history.

Often, it is the voice of the prophet, of the religious community, that tries to encourage a civilization to turn back before jumping off the economic cliff of no return. The liberation theology movement among Catholics in Latin America of the last century gave us the phrase, "God's preferential option for the poor." They noted that throughout the Old and New Testaments there was a distinct preference given to the poor by God through the prophets, apostles, and saints. For those of us in the progressive movement, this awareness of a spiritual concern for the poor can be traced to our choice to see ourselves as being connected to one another in a way that makes feeling the pain of the poor unavoidable.

We have no shortage in our time of politicians who unashamedly cite the self-centered philosophy of Ayn Rand. Rand liked to call her view "objectivism" though some liken it to libertarianism. It reminds me more of an "I got mine" philosophy than of anything else. Most of us live in a world somewhere between the extremes of absolute selfishness and absolute self-abnegation. Very few have followed the gospel imperative to "sell your possessions, and give the money to the poor" (Matt 19:21b) and, on the other hand, not many more could accurately be portrayed as being an Ebenezer Scrooge. But between the extremes of Scrooge and St. Francis there are a whole lot more people leaning towards the Scrooge end of the scale.

Because our core understanding of religious ethics is to seek the greatest good for the largest number of people, not because it is mandated in Scripture or because it is a part of a romanticized view of poverty, progressives have made a conscious choice to strive to live a life defined by radical compassion that will work to alleviate poverty. We will not silently give our consent to an economic system that unfairly, unjustly, even irrationally impoverishes the many to enrich the few. If you listen to the political rhetoric of our day, even a casual observer would conclude that Americans must hate paying taxes and that we are inclined to vilify the lazy that live off of public assistance while rarely questioning why the top 1 percent in America is taking 25 percent of the money that is being earned in our nation.[3]

Americans have an economic system that looks fair, but it is, in fact, stacked in favor of the rich. It is as if you were going to play Monopoly with three friends, but the friends started playing thirty minutes before you arrived. You play by the same rules, with the same dice and an equal buy-in from the bank, but they will have

3. Cassidy, "American Inequality."

already bought all of the assets and set up houses and hotels on the places where you will have to go. No matter how hard you work, they are going to end up with everything you have. Increasingly, our system of economics will prevent the poor from ever being able to work their way out of poverty, and it will eventually erode the middle class out of existence.

Dorothy Day, the founder of the Catholic Worker movement, preached that we need a revolution in how we think about the distribution of wealth. She said, "Our problems stem from our acceptance of this filthy, rotten system."[4] When economic commentators insist that we cannot pay a living wage to those who build, grow, or manufacture our nation's real wealth, because it would "hurt the economy" then you should immediately realize that you are reading an irrational defense of a "filthy, rotten" economic system that discourages the creation of real wealth in favor of simply transferring existing wealth into the hands of fewer and fewer people. They are asking you to accept a system in which they have already won and you have already lost before you ever get to roll your dice.

Those who resist raising the minimum wage or who insist upon legislation that undermines the unions that protect workers' jobs, wages, and benefits often cite studies that conclude that it is the greed of teachers, firefighters, labor union members, and selfish young people who want to go to college that is threatening our economic future. They use these studies, as Paul Krugman says, "the way a drunk uses a lamppost—for support not for illumination."

The stock market continues to climb to new heights, making the rich ever more rich, while real wealth remains stagnant or, in fact, declines, eroding the middle class and undermining the economic future of our nation. We have been sold a malignant myth that wealthy people are job creators. That is a ridiculous claim. Rich people don't hire new employees unless there is a consumer demand that makes having more employees profitable. Demand in the marketplace is what creates jobs, and demand comes as more people are able to buy things. Still, the far right cries out

4. Day, "On Pilgrimage."

against labor unions and against a president that they insist upon labeling "socialist," while our nation's existing wealth continues to be handed over to the super-rich and the middle class disappears before our eyes.

Naomi Klein, describing in the documentary companion to her book *The Shock Doctrine,* her important research into the rise of disaster capitalism, says:

> We are witnessing a transfer of wealth of unfathomable size. It is a transfer of wealth from the public hands, from the hands of government collected from regular people in the form of taxes, into the hands of the wealthiest corporations and individuals in the world. Needless to say, the very individuals and corporations that created this crisis.[5]

The system that is set up to enrich corporations and is controlled by the same corporations will never be able to become something that will work for the welfare of the whole nation. But what system works to create wealth and bolster the middle class? Economist Robert Reich has a very plausible answer to this question: the system employed in the United States of America between 1947 and 1977, when we built America's middle class and created the standard of living that was the envy of the world. Reich says in his documentary *Inequality for All*:

> Look back over the last hundred years and you'll see the pattern. During periods when the very rich took home a much smaller proportion of total income—as in the Great Prosperity between 1947 and 1977—the nation as a whole grew faster and median wages surged. We created a virtuous cycle in which an ever-growing middle class had the ability to consume more goods and services, which created more and better jobs, thereby stoking demand. The rising tide did in fact lift all boats.[6]

---

5. Klein, *Shock Doctrine* (Renegade Pictures, 2009).

6. Reich, *Inequality for All* (72 Productions, 2013).

Conversely, Reich points out that when we allow the greedy to control the system and grab all of the assets for themselves, the whole system crashes. He says:

> During periods when the very rich took home a larger proportion—as between 1918 and 1933, and in the Great Regression from 1981 to the present day—growth slowed, median wages stagnated and we suffered giant downturns. It's no mere coincidence that over the last century the top earners' share of the nation's total income peaked in 1928 and 2007—the two years just preceding the biggest downturns.[7]

We tend to assume that great religious leaders were all very poor and that spiritual people must therefore be suspicious of wealth. Frankly, I think that is counter to what really alleviates human suffering. Sure, if there were only a hundred apples in the world and we were only a hundred people, no one should eat ten apples. However, our problem is not that there are only one hundred apples; our situation is more that we have put a lot of apple growers out of business and fired the people who pick the apples.

While progressives do not trade in the guilt and fear of past religious eras, there is still such a thing as evil. It is evil to be so greedy that you hoard resources in a way that puts some out of work, forces others to work for poverty wages, and leaves many living on the edge of death. That's not evil because the Bible says so, even though it does; it is evil because it causes suffering.

It seems most likely to me that whatever there is of heaven and hell in the universe is what we do with this life. Therefore, having devoted ourselves to seeking the greatest good for the largest number of people, it stands to reason that we will also work to defeat, improve, or replace a system that creates widespread suffering for the comfort of a few in order to evolve toward an economy that puts people back to work and makes the basics of life available to everyone. Such a change is the only way we can keep from turning what we have of heaven into the hell on earth we do not want.

7. Ibid.

16

What Is in the Crystal Ball?

Will churches see the vision and respond to it? Some will; most will not. Many churches would, if given the choice, choose to die rather than change . . .

These faith-communities will emerge, I am confident, inside our existing structures. They will ultimately separate themselves from the pack. They will float freely, taking a wide variety of forms. They will attract the restless, the hungry, the alienated, the marginalized, the open, the honest, the doubters, the seekers. In time they will recognize kinship with one another, allowing them to coalesce and to build a new consensus.[1]

—BISHOP JOHN SHELBY SPONG

Sire, it is in truth the lot of the Church of God, in whose name I am speaking, to endure blows, and not to strike them. But also may it please you to remember that it is an anvil that has worn out many hammers.[2]

—THEODORE BEZA, SIXTEENTH-CENTURY FRENCH PROTES-TANT REFORMER

1. Spong, *A New Christianity,* 244-245.
2. Graves, "Beza."

Progressive Faith and Practice

THE FAMOUS TRAPPIST MONK Thomas Merton wrote his autobiography, *The Seven Storey Mountain*, in 1948 when he was only thirty-three years old and had been in the monastery for six or seven years. Though the book was very popular and drew attention to monastic communities all over the nation, it wasn't very many years before Merton was saying that he wished that he could gather up all of the copies and burn them.

Merton was born in France to nominally Protestant parents. His journey toward faith led him to the Catholic Church, then to monastic life, and finally to the most strict of monastic orders, the Trappists. His journey, which was profoundly intellectual while still being distinctive in its mysticism, made for a very engaging story. However, when he wrote his autobiography, Merton was still a very young man in the midst of huge life changes. His book was decidedly Roman Catholic, so much so that it was very nearly offensive to anyone who wasn't. Within a very few years, however, he became a leading world scholar in comparative religions and was in conversation with the Dalai Lama, Thich Nhat Hanh, as well as scholars of Hindu and Muslim heritage. He wrote his most famous book long before it was time to write his definitive biography.

Awareness of how unready Merton was to write *The Seven Storey Mountain* has plagued me during the writing of this book. Though I am now older than Merton lived to be, and I have delayed writing this book for some years, the movement I am trying to describe is moving and evolving so fast that it is difficult to capture the situation in print. What I know with certainty is that if I had written this book five years ago I would now be screaming more loudly about gathering all of the copies and burning them than Merton did about his autobiography. My own views and practice have evolved a great deal over the past few years, and I suspect that they will change more in the next few, but at some point the pen must drop to the page to document the process.

More than a decade ago, Bishop John Shelby Spong offered his vision for the future of the progressive church in *A New Christianity for a New World*. He predicted the emergence of new progressive faith communities that would not be a part of the old existing denominational structures and, in fact, the church where I serve as pastor is one of those new churches he foresaw.

Shortly after we first established our YouTube and iTunes channels[3] to share our weekly messages with the world, I received a call from a gentleman in Japan who asked me if I knew of any churches like ours in Japan. Sadly, I informed him that I didn't know anything about any churches of any kind in Japan. The caller was very disappointed because he assumed not only that there would be a lot of churches like ours but also he assumed that we would know each other and that there would be a network of like-minded churches.

The Center for Progressive Christianity has tried to create a directory[4] on their website, but it is not comprehensive, and many of the churches that list themselves on it are still quite traditional in their theology, though they are somewhat more open-minded about social issues such as divorce and gay marriage. Some of the self-described progressive meetings I have attended in recent years have sounded, theologically, like a Baptist summer camp meeting though they do usually boast a wonderful beer garden. But being progressive involves a great deal more than accepting our gay friends, serial monogamists, and drinking craft beer.

The original mission of the Jesus Seminar, to bring a more enlightened, progressive, and academic approach to faith into mainstream churches, has had at best only very limited success even after thirty years of impressive lectures and publications. After a century of teaching higher biblical criticism in our better seminaries and a generation of really insightful publications by John Spong, Marcus Borg, Karen Armstrong, and John Dominic Crossan, still almost all mainline denominations continue to parrot a watered-down version of a more conservative evangelical sort. They still say that Jesus is God's one and only divine Son who was killed for the forgiveness of the sins of everyone who is willing to buy into incarnational and substitutionary death theologies so

3. Community Christian Church, www.spfccc.org.
4. Center for Progressive Christianity, "Global Network."

that your as-yet-unseen eternal soul will spend eternity in an as-yet-unseen place of reward and bliss.

Many people continue to try to persuade me to accept that everyone has a right to his or her own religious opinions, and no one opinion is superior to another. This kind of religious tolerance is true enough if religion is the equivalent of choosing which color of paint you want to put on your bedroom walls. If it is simply a matter of personal taste that has nothing to do with life, health, politics, or wars then paint your room any color you like.

If, however, your religion teaches women that they are second-class citizens because they were born female, or if your religion teaches homosexuals to hate themselves, then that is a different matter. And if your religion teaches that other religions are so wrong that they are evil—evil in a way that may deserve dehumanizing treatment or even warfare—or if your religion teaches you to feel that you are broken, sinful, a worm, and to despise yourself for unavoidable human appetites, then you need to recognize that is not a matter of taste. That religion is sick.

If you are neutral about neurotic religion that provokes wars, ethnic cleansing, racial and sexual prejudice, misogyny and religious guilt, and fear, then you are not open-minded, you are just heartless, and that is nothing to be proud of. Many people try to mask moral laziness and indifference behind a facade of tolerance, but we are not doing the future any favors by pretending that this is acceptable.

There are very many good things that can come from religious education and the practice of a spiritual life, but we can't stick our heads in the sand and pretend that there are not many very damaging downsides as well. We should be civil in our engagement with traditionalists who want to keep the church mired in the Iron Age, but we should not be passive and we should not mistake cowardice for open-minded sophistication.

If the church has a future in an age of reason, we have to strengthen the good things and find ways of extinguishing the bad. Pretending that everything is just a matter of opinion and that serious scientific inquiry has the same value as wishing and magic is not helpful. We must clearly and adamantly refuse to participate in the indoctrination of another generation in the language and belief of false religion.

Still, the imminent death of old religions has been prematurely announced many times. The church has tried to silence scientists and philosophers from Galileo to Darwin, Thoreau to Sartre, but in the end the church didn't need to fight so hard. As Theodore Beza observed five hundred years ago, the church is an anvil that has worn out many hammers.

No matter how much science and technology have advanced, there is still a huge human appetite for a belief system that stands against reason and that defies rational thought and critical review. Maybe the real world is too complex, too frightening. Maybe it is just easier to have an imaginary world into which we can escape so that we don't have to feel the pain of hunger and homelessness, where we do not have to fear terrorism, war, or being made to flee our homes and become refugees. Perhaps we can placate ourselves with the slow and subtle changes that seem to nibble away at the prejudices that have plagued race relationships and even the relationships found around our holiday dinner table with gay and straight family members. We have twice elected a black president and marriage equality is spreading to even the most unlikely states. But is that enough?

Maybe we can deny the vast earth-killing pollution taking place as we burn more coal and fracture the earth harvesting natural gas because we recycle our plastic bottles and aluminum cans. It may be that the old religions of magic and superstition will die a slow death in the Americas and in Africa as it already has in Europe and most of Asia. Still, it does not seem to me that we have arrived at a place that is beyond an urgent need for the prophetic voice of reason and faith to cry out for more justice and more compassion.

I realize that my journey from the Memorial Hospital where I was born to the Memorial Gardens where my ashes will be interred is a lot closer to the ashes end of that trip than it is to the loud screaming start of my life's journey, but I feel that I have a lot more screaming yet to do. How people of faith will find one another, network, and work together in the next generation is unclear to me.

I don't know if freestanding brick-and-mortar churches will still exist a generation or two from now. I don't know if the commitment of resources and the will to keep a community alive will support much of a future for the church as we have known it. It may be that churches twenty years from now will look more like the Shriners' Mosque looks to us today—a once strong and influential institution that just seems sort of silly in the light of modern reason.

I still write columns for newspapers though fewer and fewer people read newspapers. I have now written this new book for a generation that does not often read books. I preach to fewer than one hundred people every week while thousands look in on us through the portal of their computer screens, but these viewers may never join us in putting our progressive thoughts into action.

While I am glad to have a global audience and am excited that so many look for a message of progressive faith on their computers, realistically it is the seated congregations that hire the pastors and scholars who generate that online content. If there were not a church that employed me, I would never have been able to earn the degrees or write the sermons and books that now help to feed the public's appetite for progressive religious messages. To date, every progressive congregation I know of is barely hanging on to existence, and another decade may see a sharp decline in numbers of the now retired generation that still goes to church and donates significant financial support to keep the doors open.

As I write these last lines, it is only 7°F outside. I will take food, blankets, and sleeping bags to the homeless of our city this week. Direct response to the needs of those who are in danger of freezing to death makes sense in my religion, but none of those people will be kept warm because a few thousand people have nodded in ascent to my progressive ponderings while watching one of my sermons on YouTube.

There is a profound need in our world for communities of faith to continue to exist. Clearly, most people are looking for religious instruction and inspiration on the Internet and not in brick-and-mortar churches or classrooms or from bookstores and published media. Facebook memes can have a certain cathartic satisfaction, but they are not enough to stop wars, save the earth, or solve the challenges of poverty and prejudice.

One of the heroes of the anti-war movement during the Vietnam era was Fr. Daniel Berrigan. Referencing the cross, he once said, "If you want to follow Jesus, you better look good on wood."[5] I hope that more progressive churches arise out of a shared conviction and willingness to sacrifice, as ours has. I also hope that more denominational churches will seriously choose to close the gap between what their pastors learned in graduate school and what they feel free to say in their pulpits. And I hope that progressive persons of faith will commit to a disciplined search for one another, to network with one another, to join in community action and to build new communities of faith.

I hope that new, more relevant, more prophetic and honest communities of faith will rise up from the ruins of a failed form of modern Christianity, but whether the church, as a viable institution, survives or not, persons of conscience must not stand idly by.[6]

5. Donaghy, "US Prophet."
6. Paulson, "Commencement 2011."

Bibliography

Albright, Madeline. *The Mighty and the Almighty: Reflections on America, God, and World Affairs*. New York: HarperCollins, 2006.

Amurao, Carla. "Fact Sheet: How Bad Is the School-to-Prison Pipeline?" Tavis Smiley Reports, PBS, March 26, 2013. Online: http://www.pbs.org/wnet/tavissmiley/tsr/education-under-arrest/school-to-prison-pipeline-fact-sheet/.

Baker, Alan. "Simplicity." *Stanford Encyclopedia of Philosophy*. Rev. February 25, 2010. Online: http://plato.stanford.edu/entries/simplicity/.

Barringer, Felicity. "White Roofs Catch On as Energy Cost Cutters." *New York Times*, July 29, 2009. Online: http://www.nytimes.com/2009/07/30/science/earth/30degrees.html?_r=0.

BBC News. "Penal Tour de France Pedals Off." June 4, 2009. Online: http://news.bbc.co.uk/2/hi/8082354.stm.

———. "US Guantanamo Guard Kicked Koran." June 4, 2005. Online: http://news.bbc.co.uk/2/hi/4608949.stm.

Bloy, Leon. "Musings and Thunderings of Leon Bloy." A Journey Round My Skull, December 9, 2008. Online: http://ajourneyroundmyskull.blogspot.com/2008/12/musings-and-thunderings-of-leon-bloy.html.

Borg, Marcus J. *Speaking Christian: Why Christian Words Have Lost Their Meaning and Power—and How They Can Be Restored*. New York: HarperCollins, 2011.

Botelho, Greg. "Witnesses of Florida Theater Killing Recall Flying Popcorn, Gunshot at Bail Hearing." *CNN*, February 5, 2014. Online: http://www.cnn.com/2014/02/05/justice/florida-movie-theater-shooting/.

Bunch, Will. "The World's Next Mandela Is Rotting in Jail Somewhere." *Huffington Post*, December 9, 2013. Online: http://www.huffingtonpost.com/will-bunch/worlds-next-mandela_b_4409960.html?utm_hp_ref=media&ir=Media.

Cassidy, John. "American Inequality in Six Charts." *The New Yorker*, November 2013. Online: http://www.newyorker.com/online/blogs/johncassidy/2013/11/inequality-and-growth-what-do-we-know.html.

Center for Progressive Christianity. "Global Network." Online: http://progressivechristianity.org/global-network/.

————. "A Joyful Path, Children's Curriculum Lesson Samples." Online: http://progressivechristianity.org/childrens-curriculum/childrens-progressive-christian-curriculum-sample/.

Community Christian Church of Springfield, MO. Online: https://www.youtube.com/user/CCCSpringfield and https://itunes.apple.com/us/podcast/progressive-faith-sermons/id419225485.

Cooper, John. *Panentheism: The Other God of the Philosophers.* Grand Rapids: Baker Academic, 2006.

Dawn, Marva J. *Reaching Out without Dumbing Down.* Grand Rapids: Eerdmans, 1995.

Day, Dorothy. "On Pilgrimage." *The Catholic Worker,* September 1956.

Donaghy, John. "A US Prophet." Walk the Way, May 9, 2013. Online: https://walktheway.wordpress.com/2013/05/09/a-us-prophet/.

Epstein, Isidore. *Babylonian Talmud: Tractate Shabbath.* London: Soncino, 1972.

Escamilla, Paul L. *True When Whispered: Hearing God's Voice in a Noisy World.* Nashville: Abingdon, 2010.

Esposito, John L., Darrell J. Fasching, and Todd Lewis. *World Religions Today.* New York: Oxford University Press, 2002.

Fleischer, Matthew. "US Prisons Don't Fund Education, and Everybody Pays a Price." TakePart, March 1, 2013. Online: http://www.takepart.com/article/2013/03/01/americas-inmates-education-denied-everybody-pays-price.

Freedman, Samuel. "Gay Harassment and the Struggle for Inclusion." *New York Times,* October 9, 2010. Online: http://www.nytimes.com/2010/10/09/us/09religion.html?_r=0.

Funk, Robert, and Roy Hoover. *The Five Gospels: The Search for the Authentic Words of Jesus.* San Francisco: HarperSanFrancisco, 1997.

Gandhi, Mahatma. "Prayer Is Not Asking." Online: http://www.brainyquote.com/quotes/quotes/m/mahatmagan403952.html.

Graves, Dan. "Beza, the Last of the Great Reformers." Online: http://www.christianity.com/church/church-history/timeline/1601-1700/beza-last-of-the-great-reformers-11630054.html.

Green Peace. "Koch Industries: Secretly Funding the Climate Denial Machine." Online: http://www.greenpeace.org/usa/en/media-center/reports/koch-industries-secretly-fund/.

Hansen, Grace. "Grace Hansen Quotes." Online: http://www.goodreads.com/author/quotes/6585057.Grace_Hansen.

Hedrick, Charles. *When Faith Meets Reason.* Santa Rosa, CA: Polebridge, 2008.

Hixon, Lex. *Great Swan: Meetings with Ramakrishna.* Burdett, NY: Larson, 1997.

Humphreys, Kenneth. "Nazareth—the Town that Theology Built." Online: http://www.jesusneverexisted.com/nazareth.html.

Jefferson, Thomas. *Thomas Jefferson Writings Vol. XIV.* Ulan Press, 2012.

Johnson, M. K., and Raye, C. L. "Cognitive and Brain Mechanisms of False Memories and Beliefs." In *Memory, Brain, and Belief*, edited by D. L. Schacter and E. Sarry, 35–86. Cambridge, MA: Harvard University Press.

Keck, Leander E. *The Church Confident*. Nashville: Abingdon, 1993.

Kennedy, John F. "John F. Kennedy Quotes." Online: http://www.goodreads.com/author/quotes/3047.John_F_Kennedy?page=3.

Kierkegaard, Soren. "Prayer Does Not Change God, but It Changes Him Who Prays." Online: http://www.brainyquote.com/quotes/quotes/s/sorenkierk107355.html.

————. "This Must Be Said—So Let It Be Said." Online: http://sorenkierkegaard.org/this-must-be-said-so-let-it-be-said.html.

Kirkham, Chris. "Florida Atlantic Football Stadium Will Be Named for Private Prison Company." *Huffington Post*, February 19, 2013. Online: http://www.huffingtonpost.com/2013/02/19/florida-atlantic-football-stadium_n_2720223.html.

Krugman, Paul. "Fiscal Fever Breaks." *New York Times*, December 30, 2013. Online: http://www.nytimes.com/2013/12/30/opinion/krugman-fiscal-fever-breaks.html?_r=0

Lee, Jane. "Update: Revised North Carolina Sea Level Rise Bill Goes to Governor." *Science Insider*, American Association for the Advancement of Science, July 3, 2012. Online: http://news.sciencemag.org/climate/2012/07/update-revised-north-carolina-sea-level-rise-bill-goes-governor.

Leopold, Aldo. *A Sand County Almanac*. New York: Oxford University Press, 1966.

Lowell, James. "Once to Every Man and Nation." Online: http://www.cyberhymnal.org/htm/o/n/oncetoev.htm.

Ludwig, Theodore M. *The Sacred Paths of the West*. 3rd ed. Upper Saddle River, NJ: Pearson/ Prentice Hall, 2006.

McMillan, Tom. "For 200 Years We've Been Conquering Nature." Online: http://www.brainyquote.com/quotes/quotes/t/tommcmilla170813.html.

Mirkinson, Jack. "Someone Finally Asked Malala About Drones." *Huffington Post*, November 13, 2013. Online: http://www.huffingtonpost.com/2013/11/13/cbs-malala-drones_n_4269535.html.

NAACP. "Criminal Justice Fact Sheet." Online: http://www.naacp.org/pages/criminal-justice-fact-sheet.

NASA. "Consensus: 97% of Climate Scientists Agree." Online: http://climate.nasa.gov/scientific-consensus.

Neuhaus, Richard John. *The Catholic Moment: The Paradox of the Church in the Postmodern Age*. San Francisco: Harper, 1987.

Paine, Jeffery. *Re-Enchantment: Tibetan Buddhism Comes to the West*. New York: Norton, 2004.

Paulson, Amanda. "Commencement 2011: What 10 Eminent Speakers Told Graduates." *Christian Science Monitor*. Online: http://www.csmonitor.com/USA/Education/2011/0531/Commencement-2011-what-10-

eminent-speakers-told-graduates/Elie-Wiesel-Nobel-Peace-Prize-laureate-Washington-University-in-St.-Louis.

Peck, M. Scott. *The Different Drum: Community-Making and Peace*. New York: Simon and Schuster, 1987.

Reps, Paul, and Nyogen Senzaki. *Zen Flesh Zen Bones: A Collection of Zen and Pre-Zen Writings*. Rutland, VT: Tuttle, 1998.

Rosen, Rebecca. "This Machine Surrounds Hate and Forces it to Surrender." *The Atlantic*, January 2014. Onlline: http://www.theatlantic.com/technology/archive/2014/01/this-machine-surrounds-hate-and-forces-it-to-surrender/283414/.

Russell, Bertrand. *Sceptical Essays*. New York: Routledge, 2004.

Sagan, Carl. "Encyclopaedia Galactica." Episode 12 of *Cosmos: A Personal Voyage*. PBS, December 14, 1980.

Schlesinger, Robert. "The Origins of That Eisenhower 'Every Gun That Is Made . . .' Quote." *US News & World Report*, September 30, 2011. Online: http://www.usnews.com/opinion/blogs/robert-schlesinger/2011/09/30/the-origins-of-that-eisenhower-every-gun-that-is-made-quote.

Schofield, Will. "Musings and Thunderings of Leon Bloy." Journey Round My Skull, December 9, 2008. Online: http://ajourneyroundmyskull.blogspot.com/2008/12/musings-and-thunderings-of-leon-bloy.html.

Shedd, William. "William Shedd Quotes." Online: http://www.goodreads.com/author/quotes/3878531.William_Shedd.

Sparks, Jack. *The Apostolic Fathers*. Nashville: T. Nelson, 1978.

Spong, John Shelby. *A New Christianity for a New World: Why Traditional Faith Is Dying and How a New Faith Is Being Born*. San Francisco: HarperSanFrancisco, 2001.

———. "Part IV Matthew – The Sermon on the Mount." October 24, 2013. Online: http://johnshelbyspong.com/2013/10/24/part-iv-matthew-the-sermon-on-the-mount/.

Star Wars Blog. "The StarWars.com 10: Best Yoda Quotes." Online: http://starwarsblog.starwars.com/2013/11/26/the-starwars-com-10-best-yoda-quotes/.

Steinbeck, John. *East of Eden*. New York: Viking, 1952.

Stewart, John. "Jon Stewart Quotes." Online: http://www.goodreads.com/author/quotes/466.Jon_Stewart?page=1.

Swimme, Brian, and Thomas Berry. *The Universe Story: From the Primordial Flaring Forth to the Ecozoic Era—A Celebration of the Unfolding of the Cosmos*. San Francisco: HarperSanFrancisco, 1992.

Symphony of Science. "A Wave of Reason." Online: https://www.youtube.com/watch?v=1PT9odAA49Q.

Thompson, Hunter. "Hunter S. Thompson Quotes." Online: https://www.goodreads.com/author/quotes/5237.Hunter_S_Thompson.

Tillich, Paul, *Systematic Theology*. 3 vols. Chicago: University of Chicago Press, 1951–63.

Trounstine, Jean. "The Battle to Bring Back Pell Grants." *Boston Magazine*, March 4, 2013. Online: http://www.bostonmagazine.com/news/ blog/2013/03/04/the-battle-to-bring-back-pell-grants-for-prisoners/.

Tyson, Neil deGrasse. "We Are All Connected." Online: https://www.youtube. com/watch?v=CtWB90bVUO8.

UPI. "Harvard Study: Iraq/Afghan War Tab \$4T–\$6T." March 29, 2013. Online: http://www.upi.com/Top_News/US/2013/03/29/Harvard-study-IraqAfghan-war-tab-4T-6T/UPI-70971364571298/.

USA Today. "Guard Convicted of Urinating on Inmates." Online: http:// usatoday30.usatoday.com/tech/news/techinnovations/2003-06-05-urine-trouble_x.htm.

Ward, Katie, et al. "Incarceration within American and Nordic Prisons: Comparison of National and International Policies." Engage. Online: http://www.dropoutprevention.org/engage/incarceration-within-american-and-nordic-prisons/.

Washington's Blog. "Japan Reacts to Fukushima Crisis by Banning Journalism." November 27, 2013. Online: http://www.washingtonsblog.com/2013/11/ japan-reacts-fukushima-crisis-banning-journalism.html.

Watts, Alan. *Eastern Wisdom, Modern Life: Collected Talks 1960–1980.* New World Library, 2006.

———. "Music and Life." Online: http://www.youtube.com/ watch?v=fbGYKKLco0Q.

Welch, Kelly. "Howard Zinn's Critical Criminology: Understanding His Criminological Perspective." *Contemporary Justice Review* 12/4 (2009) 485–503.

Wikipedia. "Unites States Armed Forces." Online: http://en.wikipedia.org/wiki/ United_States_Armed_Forces.

Wing, Nick. "Here Are All of the Nations That Incarcerate More of Their Population than the U.S." *Huffington Post*, August 13, 2013. Online: http://www.huffingtonpost.com/2013/08/13/incarceration-rate-per-capita_n_3745291.html.

Young, Angelo. "And the Winner for the Most Iraq War Contracts Is . . . KBR, with \$39.5 Billion in a Decade." *International Business Times*, March 19, 2013. Online: http://www.ibtimes.com/winner-most-iraq-war-contracts-kbr-395-billion-decade-1135905.

Zinn, Howard. "Three Holy Wars." *Democracy Now*, January 8, 2010. Online: http://www.democracynow.org/blog/2010/1/8/howard_zinn_three_holy_wars.